invisible
shadows

A black woman's life
in Nova Scotia

Verna Thomas

Nimbus Publishing Limited
PO Box 9166
Halifax, NS
B3K 5M8
(902) 455-4286

Printed and bound in Canada
Design: Kathy Kaulbach,
Paragon Design Group

National Library of Canada
Cataloguing in Publication Data

    Thomas, Verna, 1935-
    Invisible shadows : a Black
    woman's life in Nova Scotia
    ISBN 1-55109-393-6

1. Thomas, Verna, 1935- . 2. Black Canadian women—Nova Scotia—Biography. 3. Racism—Nova Scotia. 4. Nova Scotia—Race relations. I. Title.

Image Sources: "Hants County," p.3, Bob Brooks Coll., PANS; "Harvesting apples," p.4, NS Info Service, PANS; "Churchill Shipyards," p.12, PANS; "Moirs Ltd. Halifax," p.60, NS Info Service, PANS; "Stag Inn sign," p.70, PANS; "Stag Inn," p.71, PANS; "Oxmobile," p.77, PANS; "Certificate of freedom," p.82, PANS; "Halifax Public Gardens," p.89, NS Info Service, PANS; "Africville," p.90, Bob Brooks Coll, PANS; "Cornwallis Street Baptist Church," p.105, Acadia University Archives; "Baptist Church," p.107, PANS; "River Baptism," p.110, Acadia University Archives. All other photographs are the author's own.

FC2350.B6Z7 2002   305.48'8960716092   C2002-900125-0
F1038.T48A3 2002

Canadä   The Canada Council | Le Conseil des Arts
                 for the Arts | du Canada

We acknowledge the financial support of the Government of Canada through the Book Publishing Industry Development Program (BPIDP) and the Canada Council for our publishing activities.

Contents

Acknowledgements iv

Preface v

Foreword by George Elliott Clarke vi

Introduction 1

Part 1: Mount Denson 3

Part 2: Preston 69

Appendix A 181

Dedicated to the memory of my late parents,
William and Sarah States,
and my late husband,
John Edward Thomas Jr.

Acknowledgements

Acknowledging every individual who in some way contributed to the writing of this book is impossible, but I would especially like to recognize those who through overt acts of kindness and expressions of confidence supported its completion.

To those I interviewed who were concerned that the history of Preston be written and those who trusted me to give an honest account of it, I am greatly indebted: James Colley, Mary Glasgow-Colley, Charles Glasgow, Mae Kane, Madeline Kane, Kathleen Thomas, John and Dorothy Williams, Alice Williams, and Paula Williams. Also, those now deceased: Myrtle Bundy, Alice Brooks, Albert and Blanche Crawley, John Crawley, Bernard Cain, James Cain, William and Florence Diggs, James Slawter, Susana Smith, Rebecca Smith, and Fred Thomas.

Thank you to Trevor Green, whose drawing appears on page 169. To Jessie Tellez, I owe an incredible debt of gratitude for her unwavering encouragement, her many, many hours spent on the computer, her trips to Preston, and her persistent quote, "Verna, you're getting there." In more ways than one she made writing this book not only possible but necessary.

I would also like to thank Dorothy Blythe and Sandra McIntyre at Nimbus Publishing for bringing enthusiasm and constructive criticism to the manuscript.

Finally, I owe a debt of gratitude to my family: Wendell, Miles, Cordell and Evetta, Wanda, Tina, and Wendy and Victor, and my grandchildren, Natalie, Germaine, Nadine, Jillian, Cordell Jr., Dayne, Nicole, and Natasha. They endured the writing of this book and adjusted their lives to my erratic schedule. I am particularly grateful for their insistent question, "Have you finished yet?"

I wish to acknowledge the financial assistance of Heritage Canada.

Preface

From the time my late husband, John, and I took our many walks through the desolate areas of Preston, the idea for this book emerged. As we strolled along the unused roads of lower Brian Street and the old Crawley Road, I became dazzled by the sparkling lakes and the beautiful flowers that grew wild. Everywhere we turned we found old stone foundations, wells, stone markers, and tombstones. These surroundings brought Preston's past alive and fed my desire to someday write about this unique community.

Very little has been written about the experiences of Black Canadians, much less about the experiences of Black Nova Scotians— how they climbed out of the bondage of slavery, isolation, exploitation, and neglect and what effect that process continues to have on those who live in the province today, especially in all-black communities like Preston. This book is my discovery of our lived history, not a picture of how other people want black life to be. I hope to give the reader some understanding of the uniqueness and significance of the Black community in Nova Scotia, and not to idealize what was in fact a life of social deprivations.

All incidents recounted here are based on the journals I have kept throughout my life, as well as newspaper clippings. To have heard the past unfold by word of mouth from Preston elders such as Susanna Smith ("Mum Suze"), John Crawley, Alice Brooks, Bernard Cain, Albert and Blanche Crawley, Gertrude Crawley, Myrtle Bundy, and many others has been invaluable to my understanding of our history.

It was never my intention to write a memoir, but because records of black history are few, lacking in detail, and obscure, and because ours is primarily an oral tradition, my research is interwoven with personal experience. Also, being black and growing up in a predominantly white community, then moving to a predominantly black one, has given me a unique perspective on the problems created by racism throughout Nova Scotia's history. Mine is, of course, just one story of many.

Foreword

Visible Enlightenment: Introducing Verna Thomas

Verna Thomas is one of those secret treasures—or weapons—that the Black Nova Scotian—or "Africadian"—community just keeps on hoarding. I mean, she seems to be—to the unwary—another of those estimable, stylish, demure church ladies, crowned with a dignified—no, indignant—hat, who always has a spiritual, or scripture, or a smile, gracing her lips. She may not seem, at first glance, interested or engaged by the secular, the worldly, the mundane. But Verna Thomas is a roots intellectual, a wisdom woman, a politic philosophe. She is one of those indomitable women who surveys and scrutinizes, excoriates and condemns, laughs and satirizes, while sitting and having a piece of toast and a cup of tea, or while standing haughtily on the steps of a church, or while exchanging gossip—gospel, really—with scintil-latingly critical friends. We Black Nova Scotians—Africadians, I say, Africadians—are lucky, blessed, by the presence of women community thinkers, gifted with exegetical insight, forensic knowledge, and inex-haustibly righteous—and right-on—vocabularies. Verna Thomas is the latest of these Africadian womanists to 'speak truth to power'—but she is still among the few to put her utterance on paper.

Ms. Thomas descends—I witness—from a proud line of Africadian belles-lettristes. Her autobiography follows journalist Carrie Best's That Lonesome Road (1977), centenarian Ethel Gibson's My Journey to Eternity (1988), and poet Grace Lawrence's Reflections to the Third Power (1989). Where Ms. Thomas ventures into community cum church history, she follows the examples of pioneer historian Pearleen Oliver's A Brief History of the Colored Baptists of Nova Scotia (1953), activist Edith Cromwell's Inglewood My Community (1993), Cherry M. Paris's Windsor

Plains United Baptist Church: A Brief History (2001), and retired teacher Donna Byard Scaley's excellent *Colored Zion: The History of Zion United Baptist Church* (2001).

Ms. Thomas's work is also a capital example of the spontaneous remembering and recovery of personal lives and community histories that characterize so much of the writing that gets done—mainly by women—in the historical African-Canadian communities. *Invisible Shadows: A Black Woman's Life in Nova Scotia* sits well beside Cheryl Foggo's *Pourin' Down Rain* (1990), her memoir about growing up black in 1950s-1960s Calgary, Alberta; Carol Talbot's *Growing up Black in Canada* (1984), which tells of the author's post-war girlhood in Windsor, Ontario; Karen Shadd-Evelyn's *I'd Rather Live in Buxton* (1993), her memoir about life in that Afro-Ontario community; and then such histories as Dorothy Shreve's *Pathfinders of Liberty and Truth: A Century with the Amherstburg Regular Missionary Baptist Association* (1990) and the *Window of Our Memories* (1981, 1990), a two-volume oral history of Black Prairie settlers assembled by Velma Carter, Leah Carter, and Wanda Akili. Verna Thomas traverses the same historical/theological ground as her 'indigenous' African-Canadian foremothers and contemporary sisters.

In African-American literature, the popular autobiographies are generally by men: spiritual/political leaders, sports heroes, celebrated musicians, ex-cons, and, now and then, writers (Richard Wright, James Baldwin, etc.). In African-Canadian literature, though, most of the autobiographies have been penned by women—the 'church ladies,' to be precise. Their narratives treat social struggle and moral uplift, but with great complexity. Their themes acquire equal textures of comic levity and tragic depth because of the varying stances and strategies they use to confront the demon, '(white) racism,' and its *doppelgänger*, 'male chauvinism.'

Verna Thomas appreciates the double nature of her task. In her own riff on W.E.B. Du Bois's famous formulation of "double-consciousness" in his classic, African-American autobiography-and-sociological study, *The Souls of Black Folk* (1902), she discusses her own development of "double vision" as a consequence of racism: "to be black, you have to live in two worlds, play by two sets of rules, and struggle to maintain your sanity when these two realities collide." Ms. Thomas learns that "The colour bar meant that black people were barred from everything except the barnyard." She asserts that, "As a black woman, I found myself part of a society that didn't see me as a woman, but rather as a colour." Hired as a domestic by one white woman, Ms. Thomas is not treated as a 'sister' but as a slave, and so, bravely, proudly, she quits. (Such personal acts of resistance are inspiringly frequent in Ms. Thomas's account of her life.) Joyously married to John Thomas as an interventionist mother and inventive homemaker, Ms. Thomas insists, even so, on finishing high school, taking university courses, and having a career, despite her husband's thought that she "was stepping out of line...." Ms. Thomas says "there was no such thing as a feminist consciousness-raising group" in the Africadian community of Preston when she moved there in the mid-twentieth century. But there was a tradition of *de facto* black women's leadership and independent thought—i.e. 'womanism,' a philosophy summed up in Ms. Thomas's attractive declaration, "It has never been my style to take cheap grace and quick answers."

But Verna Thomas's "double vision" did not only result from racism and sexism. Impressively, and originally, she analyzes her socio-political and psychological condition from the point of being "a half-breed outsider," a so-called "yellow-face," a brown-skinned, semi-Mi'kmaq, semi-Irish black woman from a multi-racial, pastoral community in the Annapolis Valley, who has undertaken to 'immigrate to' wholly black-identified Preston, a hard-scrabble homeland enduring the worst excesses of Nova Scotian *apartheid*. While never relinquishing her objective, 'outsider' vision, Ms. Thomas is able to peer intimately, subjectively, into the community experience, to understand its inextinguishable pride, its vaulted hostilities, and its social contradictions. She trains a similarly scholarly eye on "Black" Halifax and the now-desecrated oasis of Africville, determining their strengths and their sorrows.

One must not read *Invisible Shadows* merely for its social science insights, for that would be like ignoring jewels to study their velvet display backgrounds instead. Verna Thomas is a speaker-writer, and her text showcases the most interesting *orature*. Here grandparents are "Grampy" and "Grammy"; children turned "bottom-up" end up with tingly "backsides"; bantam hens are "as sassy as a blue-ass fly"; the author falls and strikes her head so hard on ice "I could smell my brains"; and some folks turn "half-sideways" because they feel cross and evil. The language is homely and comely, all at—intoxicatingly—once.

To describe every life as a journey is a grand cliché. Yet, Verna Thomas has lived an odyssey—from the Annapolis Valley to Preston, from Africville to Africa. One of her ex-slave ancestors who settled in the Annapolis Valley was named "Jobe"; so named too is the tour guide who takes her to Anse St. Bernard, in Dakar, Africa, the departure point for so many Africans sold into slavery in the Americas so long ago. In her quests for self-actualization and self knowledge, Ms. Thomas bridges, virtually, the pre-slavery and post-slavery Africadian worlds. She knows that "my roots were my destiny." It is a visible enlightenment.

George Elliott Clarke

University of Toronto
Toronto, Ontario

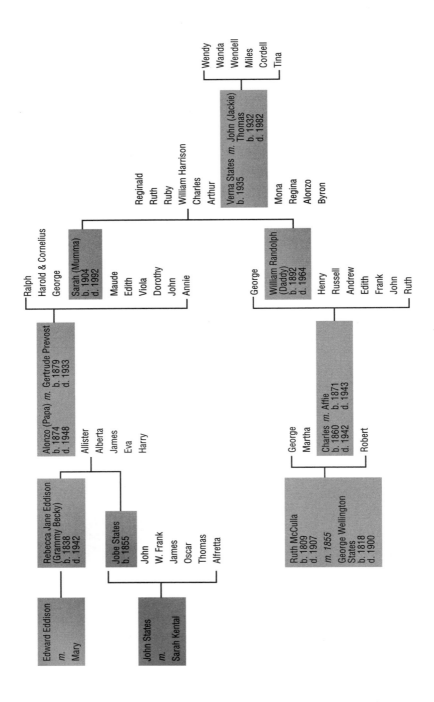

Introduction

I am a Canadian woman of African, Irish, and Native descent, born in 1935 in the month of May. Not the first or the middle of the month, no, not me. I waited until the thirtieth to make my entrance into the world. I grew up black in the white community of Mount Denson in Nova Scotia. I grew up knowing I was black, but I didn't notice being treated any differently than the other children in the community. I had no racial consciousness as a child and no interest in learning about my motherland—I didn't know there was any such place. My awakening consciousness of race and racism came when I left home, ingrained with behaviour and ideals that approximated those of the white race more than they did my own, to live in Preston, a place where people breathed in racism from the day of their birth.

When I moved to Preston and started looking for work in Halifax County, I was confronted with a discrimination that created frustration and insecurity within me. Suddenly, I had the feeling that I had been raised in a world of make-believe, that the peaceful, understanding world of my youth had been a dream. I got little support for the bewilderment and hurt I felt as I came smack up against this different world. Coming face to face with racism gave me double vision: how can I fully trust white people and where are my people when I need them most? I felt doomed. Of course, even those black people who grew up surrounded by racism were not born expecting it. Black people are not presented with a handbook to prepare us for racism's confining, confusing rules. No, the humiliating system of discrimination creeps up on a person day after day.

To some, we have come a very long way from slavery to freedom. To others, we have come a long way from slavery but still have a way to go to freedom. My race claimed a major victory when the chains of slavery were cut from our ancestors' ankles and they led us—their descendants—out of bondage. These were industrious, hard-working people who struggled to build the foundation of a black community that would pass from generation to generation in Nova Scotia. When I look at how far my people have come as members of strong and viable communities that continue to claim the rights of all Canadians, I feel we have a long way to go yet. Even in this new millennium, we are still very much dependent on government handouts and special programs, "solutions" that feed into segregation and social isolation.

As a result of writing this book, I have learnt how important it is to take time out to look back and reflect on the past. A greater awareness of my environment grew within me as I delved into the mystery of how the two widely different cultures I come from were created. I have come to realize just how much I have altered my Mount Denson lifestyle in an attempt to fit into the way of life in Preston. Because my father was never unemployed and my mother held paying jobs outside the home, my family always lived a notch or two above poverty. I never turned down a chance to get ahead in life by despairing because I'm black. But when I came to Preston, my eyes had their first glimpse of a bigger picture—the social struggle that has historically divided whites and blacks in Nova Scotia, in Canada, and across the continent. And I found a community of descendants of the province's original settlers: a people isolated, locked into a subculture of poverty, holding onto their fear and mistrust in white people. While writing this book I felt myself sharing the hardships, insecurities and determination which often accompanied the stories told to me by community residents, past and present. Writing is just one of the many ways in which I have tried to inspire others to let go of their fears and participate fully in society.

Oftentimes my dreams carry me back home, to waking early in the morning when the fields, the fruit trees and grass were mysteriously still, as if still sleeping. I would lie there in bed with a head full of picture-perfect adventures for the day. Suddenly, the sound of Mr. Riley's tractor would break that peaceful silence and I would think, "Oh dear! Another day in the life of this little farming community." Mount Denson takes its name from Colonel Henry Denny Denson, one of the original Irish settlers and proprietors of West Falmouth in the 1700s. Today, Mount Denson is a little farming village nestled between the towns of Hantsport and Windsor in the beautiful Annapolis Valley, widely known for its apple industry. This is where I grew up. Wherever you look, nature is profuse with its blessings, from the apple orchards

The picturesque Annapolis Valley—home of my childhood.

to the corn fields. Just about every little piece of land in the valley has an apple tree or some fruit tree on it.

The history of fruit trees in Mount Denson began in the 1700s when the Acadians planted the first apple trees in the rich soil of the valley. From then, it was evident to the Acadian farmers that the climate and fertile land were suitable for the production of fruit. A French census of 1698 records 1,584 apple trees growing at Port Royal, Annapolis Valley in the gardens of fifty-four families. After the 1713 Treaty of Utrecht, Great Britain formally took possession of Nova Scotia and developed a lively trade with the Acadian farmers. Apples were a vital part of the food supply for both sides.

Besides the abundant apple tree, pear, cherry, plum, and quince trees also grew in valley orchards.

When the British lost in the American War of Independence (1775-83), many supporters, known as United Empire Loyalists, had no option but to move away. Some twenty-eight thousand Loyalists came to Nova Scotia at that time, some to the Annapolis Valley. In the late 1700s the apple orchards were on their way to becoming an apple-producing centre. In the War of 1812, as in the American War of Independence, black refugees were given their freedom in Canada and many came to Nova Scotia. People from other nations—Scotland, Ireland and Germany—came to the valley as well.

Farming and the promise of land attracted new settlers, including my great great grandparents, who arrived in the mass migration in 1815 of Chesapeake Blacks to Nova Scotia. Three years after their arrival,my great-grandfather on my father's side, George Wellington States, was born in Mount Denson of free slaves. On September 3,

1855, he married Ruth McCulla, an immigrant born in Belfast, Ireland. Her family had possibly come to Nova Scotia after one of the potato famines. On December 25, 1877, after having lived in Mount Denson for some years as the only mixed-race family, my great grand-parents purchased a one-acre plot of land in Mount Denson from Charles Akins for the sum of fifty dollars. Our family name was among the earliest Mount Denson settlers and it remains there still.

Great-grandfather States planted some fruit trees and farmed his land for a living. My great grandparents had four children: George, Martha, Charles (Grampy Charlie) and Robert. I don't know much else about great-grandfather George and grandmother Ruth because in my day, grown-ups didn't tell tales and stories about their family in the presence of children. However, life for them as a mixed couple with mulatto children in Mount Denson must have been somewhat comfortable because their son Charles and his family remained in Mount Denson.

My great-great grandfather on Mumma's side, John States, mar-ried Sarah Kental and they had seven children: Jobe, John, W. Frank, James, Oscar, Thomas and Alferetta. They lived on the Bog Road in

Alonzo States (Papa), ca. 1942. Papa always wore his brown felt hat when he dressed up.

Grammy Gertie, ca. 1929
I never knew her but was
told she couldn't sing. One
day while she sat outside
singing her baby to sleep, a
neighbour thought she was
crying in pain and came to
check on her.

Falmouth. Jobe, my great grandfather, married Rebecca Jane Eddison, who was born on July 1, 1838 to Edward and Mary Eddison. She was the granddaughter of John Eddison, a former cotton plantation slave in the American South. Grammy Becky, known to most in Hants and Kings counties as "Aunt Becky," lived in a small house on Schurman Road in Mount Denson. She and great-grandfather Jobe had six children: Alonzo (Papa), Allister, Alberta, James, Eva and Harry.

For generations fruit growing was a thriving business in the valley. By the year 1900, outside apple pickers were brought in because apple crops were too large for families to handle alone. During the apple-picking season, the apple growers would hire twenty-five to thirty pickers at a time and house them in the bunkhouses on their property. They gave the pickers their meals, lodging, and a dollar a day for picking apples and filling the barrels. Men from the French Shore, Yarmouth County, and Preston came to the valley for the season. During this time of prosperity in the valley my maternal grandfather, Alonzo States, who we called Papa, worked with the power company putting in power poles and checking the power lines. Born in Mount Denson in 1874, Papa married Gertrude Prevost on January 12, 1898. They lived in Windsor Plains and had ten children: Ralph, Harold and Cornelius (twins), George, Sarah (Mumma), Maude, Edith, Viola,

Dorothy, John, and Annie. My grandparents were well respected in the community of Windsor Plains. Grammy Gertie, who was born in 1879, was a sickly woman. My mother, Sarah (the eldest daughter), helped her father take care of the children until she married Daddy. Grammy Gertie spent the last two years of her life confined to her bed. She died October 15, 1933 and her funeral was held at her home on Panuke Road, Windsor Plains. Papa remained in their homestead with his remaining children until his death on January 7, 1948.

Charles States, my paternal grandfather, was born on April 24, 1860 in Mount Denson. On September 7, 1889 he married Alferetta States, who was born in 1871, and they had nine children: George, William (my father), Henry, Russell, Andrew, Edith, Frank, John, and Ruth. By the time I came into this world, only Russ, Andrew, Edith, Frank and my father were alive. Grampy Charlie worked at the ship

Grampy Charlie and Grammy Affie, beside their home, ca. 1939. Grampy and Grammy could send us on errands and discipline us just like Daddy and Mumma.

building yards. He died March 6, 1942. Grammy Affie died less than a year later on January 8, 1943.

Even the Depression years were not terribly hard on the valley. It was said that apple prices were steady and the apple industry was more prosperous during the thirties than at any other period. As the 1930s ended, so did the apple industry's growth period. In 1939, apple growers were still looking toward Great Britain as the buyer for most of their fruit. However, World War Two called an abrupt halt to nearly all shipments of apples. Thus, farmers switched from the overseas trade to selling apples and their by-products in the Atlantic Canadian market. The apple by-products industry, with cannery plants in Hantsport, Kings County, and throughout the valley, soon became big business. Canned apple sauce, other canned fruit, and a variety of fruit juices kept the apple industry alive.

There were only a half dozen black families in Mount Denson. Of those, four had children and two didn't. Three of the homes that had children were found in an approximately twenty-acre radius of the beginning of Shore Road (renamed Mckinlay). Shore Road led to everything. From Windsor along the main highway through Falmouth into Mount Denson, a right turn leads onto Shore Road. The first house on the right-hand side of this road was mine, where the ten of us lived. Next on the right was Grampy Charlie and Grammy Affie's house, where my Uncle Frank, Aunt Eunice (who was white), and their six children lived. Uncle Frank had a strawberry patch; we kids used to help him and Aunt Eunice pick and box the strawberries to sell. Uncle Frank often came over on the step to talk to Daddy on some long evenings. He used to get his water from our well. Sometimes he would drop in for a cup of tea before getting a pail of water in the morning. He continued to do this even after Daddy's death.

On the left-hand side of the road across from Grampy's, Uncle Russ, Aunt Elta, and their sixteen children lived. Uncle Russ used to come to our house to listen with Daddy to the fights on the radio. He was a very pleasant and friendly man and would always take time out to tell us a funny little story or do something to make us laugh. When their home burnt down one year, Aunt Elta came to stay with us.

Although I was small, I can still remember her getting up early in the morning to make tea biscuits for us kids.

Just down from them Uncle Andrew lived alone. When my brother, Chum was nine or ten years old, he went to live at Uncle Andrew's house. Mumma did Chum's and Uncle Andrew's laundry and some cooking for them. We spent a lot of time at Uncle Andrew's because he brought us the kind of treats we wanted. He also let us do some cooking for him, which we messed up most of the time. One winter night, my sister Mona and I decided to treat him to some home-made ice-cream. I washed the ice-cream churn out with warm water and lots of sunlight soap. Mona put the ingredients into the clean churn. We put the churn into a pan of snow and we both churned the ice-cream to a high peak. We put the churn outside in the snow. It smelled good—a real strawberry smell—and it looked very tasty in our bowls. Be that as it may, when we took our first spoonful it was so soapy tasting I am sure bubbles were coming from our mouths.

The States men, like the men in many other families in the community, made their living working in the shipyards and pulp mill in Hantsport and on farms throughout the area. Uncle Andrew worked at the mill with Daddy until 1957 when he moved to Calgary, Alberta.

Daddy's sister Edith and her husband William Tyler lived on Apple Tree Road. They had one adopted son. When Aunt Edith was nine years old, she hurt her hip coasting and ever after walked with a limp. Sometimes when Uncle Bill was going into Hantsport with his horse and wagon, he dropped Aunt Edith off at our house and picked her up on the way back home. Grammy Becky, Papa's mother, lived alone. She used to walk down to our house. We could see her walking over the hill by Mr. Allies'—a white neighbour—and we would go to the corner to meet her. When she got to our house, she would always stop in the front and look at Mumma's flower garden and pay special attention to the bleeding hearts. She liked to take her cane and loosen the soil around the bleeding heart plant.

My father, William Randolph States, was born in Mount Denson. He was known throughout Hants and Kings counties as Will. His childhood was spent playing around the green fields and beautiful fruit orchards of Mount Denson. Aunt Eva often told us how she took Daddy by the hand to and from school. Although he only went to grade five or six before leaving school to go to work with his father, his spelling and reading were good and he was a beautiful writer. He was a lover of horses and when he grew up, he owned a beautiful riding horse and carriage. Many Sunday afternoons he would dress in his finest, hitch his horse to the carriage, and ride to Windsor Plains to attend church. It was during his visits to Windsor Plains that he met his bride-to-be—Sarah Jane States. A small woman of ninety-eight pounds, my mother was kept busy caring for her sick mother and nine other siblings for much of her youth. However, she must have found time to spend with my father, though I don't know just how long their courtship lasted. On December 13, 1922, two days after Daddy's thirtieth birthday, he and Mumma got married. They lived in a big old house by the railroad track on the Shore Road in Mount Denson. That's where they lived until their third child was born; then they built our present home on the Shore Road, next to Grammy Affie and Grampy Charlie.

Daddy was an upright, honest and sincere man of character who rarely socialized. It seemed as if he was always coming from or going

Daddy (at left), with Mr. Allison, 1959. Special occasions were the only times Daddy dressed in his navy blue suit and didn't wear his cap.

invisible shadows

to work. He got pleasure from listening to the Joe Louis fights and the "Amos and Andy Show" on the radio. He worked at both Hantsport shipyards earning a living for his family.

Mumma was a hard-working woman. With children as curious and as poky as me, I know she was kept very busy. She kept us nice and clean, always had well-prepared meals, and had the dining room table set three times every day. She was very protective of us but stern. She said what she meant and meant what she said. If for some reason we refused to obey her, we were turned bottom-up. Believe me, when Mumma turned us upright we had a stingy bottom for a while. Of course during the thirties and forties strict discipline was as much a part of the Mount Denson climate as the weather.

In the thirties and forties, the farmers in the valley laboured from dawn to sunset and didn't need an alarm clock to wake them in the morning; the crowing of the rooster took care of that. They were off to the barns to milk and feed the cows before sunup. They also fed the horses, pigs, chickens, geese, ducks, turkeys, and lambs. Newborns, including calves, foals, and piglets, were given special care. During chicken-production days the farmers checked the pasture and fields regularly to see if any hens were setting there. Some hens went to the

Mumma at her 76th birthday party, 1980. She is holding the money doll I made her—a dollar for every year. She thought highly of my gift and never removed a dollar from it.

Churchill Shipyards, launching of the ship *Forest*, ca. 1872. (Oil on canvas, artist unknown.) Local men, including my father, helped build and repair ships at shipyards such as this one in Hantsport.

pasture or field, prepared a grass nest, laid their eggs, and sat on them until they hatched. The hens then led their chicks back to the coop.

Farming was the main source of income for the residents of Mount Denson. However, not every family had a large farm and supplementary work was sought in the bordering town of Hantsport. Daddy was one man who found work there. In 1907, at the age of fifteen, he took his first job with his father at the shipyards. Up until 1920, Hantsport's economy depended greatly on the building and repairing of wooden ships. There were two shipyards in Hantsport: Churchill and David North. Some of the most seaworthy ships that sailed the sea were built at Churchill Shipyards, like the *Avon*, referred to as the "Queen of the River." Some of the wooden ships used as gypsum carriers—*Plymouth, Hamburg, Bristol* and *Ontario*—were built in Hantsport at the J.B. North Shipyard. In the late 1800s and early 1900s, Hantsport, one of the world's few natural dry docks, rivalled the largest shipping ports in the world. It had many gypsum ships come in to dock. The ships would come up on the flood tide, in from the Bay of Fundy, up the Minas Channel to Minas Basin and into the

invisible shadows

loading dock at Hantsport. The ships docked exactly three hours before high tide because they had to sail at high tide and it took three hours to load the gypsum.

When Daddy went to work at the Churchill Shipyards in Hantsport, he began to learn about machinery and building things. He put some of this ship-building knowledge into the construction of a model ship. The model was about three feet long and four feet high, a beautiful piece of work that sat over the top of our cellar steps. When I was young, I often wished this model ship could be placed in a museum to be seen by many other people. It disappeared one day in the early 1980s. To this day, I am still hopeful that it will be returned to our family.

The days of the wooden ships drew to an end during World War One, and Hantsport's survival became a struggle when the Churchill Shipyards closed in 1927. Between those struggling years of 1920 and 1927, Daddy worked on large farms in Mount Denson. He was up early in the morning to go to the farmer's barns to milk the cows. Then he came home for breakfast before going back to the farmyards to complete his day's work. This was a time when he stoned a lot of wells in Hantsport, Falmouth, and Mount Denson for the residents of those communities. He kept himself busy earning a living for his family.

In March 1927, R. A. Joudrey, Charles Wright, and T. B. Akin changed the economic outlook of Hantsport with the founding of the Minas Basin Pulp and Power Company Limited. The pulp mill was built on the former Churchill Shipyards site. R. A. Joudrey hired Daddy to work at this mill. Over his many years of work at the mill, Daddy learned about every machine there. Whenever something went wrong with any of the machines, Daddy seemed to know just what to do. He could be referred to as a technical engineer in his own right and was a member of the Brotherhood of Pulp and Sulpherite Workers, local 304. Every day Daddy was seen walking over the hill to and from work, with his lunch-can in his hand. We children took turns checking his can as he always left a cookie or piece of cake in it for us. There wasn't anything better than opening the lunch can and finding a piece of Mumma's frosted layer cake inside. We knew our taste buds were in for a fine treat then!

In every backyard stood a sawhorse and chopping block. The smell of fresh-sawed wood filled the air as the men sawed and chopped wood into stove-length pieces. They piled it into heaps along the side of the woodshed to season (dry). Once seasoned, the wood was carried into the woodshed and piled up for firewood. Daddy and the other men took great pride in their wood yard. After sawing and splitting the logs, he would rake all the wood chips into a pile. The chips were great for starting a good fire in the kitchen stove.

During the winter, trees were cut down when the wood was drier and empty of sap. At the end of the winter when the snow crust was on top of the deep snow, we could walk on the crust and it was easier for the horse and sled team to haul the timber and firewood out of the woods. The man of the house had to spend many hours chopping down trees. Daddy was no exception. He spent many long, cold hours in the woods. The woodsmen built log cabins in the woods where four or five of them could cook and find shelter. These cabins were known as lumber camps. Once the men got into the woods, they stayed in their cabin if a storm came up. Sometimes this meant staying all night until the storm passed over.

Once Daddy failed to remain in the cabin. He never forgot the experience. They were miles back into the woods, chopping firewood when a heavy snow storm began. By afternoon a severe blizzard was blowing. When dusk came that night Daddy's mind fell on Mumma at home alone with small children on a stormy night. By nightfall he wanted to leave the camp for home. Against his brother's wishes and in the face of a dreadful winter blizzard, Daddy was determined to go home. With such great determination he set out, his brother following him. Try as they might to struggle through the storm, the freezing snow got the best of them. Daddy's feet became so cold they went numb. He was overcome and fell into the snow. His brother managed to drag him to an old barn nearby where they spent the night, suffering from the cold and with aching feet.

Upon their return home the next day, the doctor was called in to take a look at Daddy's feet. (In those days the doctors made home visits. At any hour of the day or night you could call a doctor in. He was an integral part of the community life.) They had been so frozen that surgery had to be done. Daddy went next door to Grampy's house and, sitting in the big armchair in Grammy's living room chewing on a plug of Club tobacco, he watched the doctor amputate two of his toes. Daddy didn't take time out for recovery. The toes were not healed before he was hard at it again.

Lumbermen went into the woods to cut logs for timber and firewood. Some of them spent the winter there in the lumber camps. In early spring, when ice pellets melted in the Avon River, we saw the wood cutters coming out of the woods. When they came out in the spring carrying their large knapsacks on their backs, their unshaved faces and untidy appearance made them look like "tramps," which is exactly what they were called. When we saw one of these lumbermen or so-called tramps, we ran for miles. It was our fear that tramps and gypsies took little children away.

After the long walk along the one-lane logging road out of the woods, the tramps were hungry and would stop at people's homes asking for something to eat. One spring day, just as Mumma was taking a loaf of bread out of the oven, placing it on the small table in the kitchen, buttering the top and leaving it to cool, a lumberman came to her door for a bit to eat. After he finished his meal, which included the home-made bread, he must have thought she had take-out service, because a short while after he left, Mumma discovered a loaf of bread missing off the small table. This theft was unusual as up to then nobody had ever taken anything from another's home. Everyone could go to their neighbour's house and everyone left their doors unlocked.

During the 1930s, the Great Depression era, both men and women worked hard to eke out a living. I grew up when times were plain and very simple. Money was important, yet money was not the all-in-all. During those simple times, people didn't dwell on the things they didn't have but rather made good of the things they did have. There was no inside plumbing so Daddy and my older brothers carried in pails of water from the well from the backyard. The women had big narrow copper boilers that they put on their stoves to heat water for washing. Every Monday, Wednesday and Friday morning we awoke to the sound of water pouring from the water pails into the boilers on the stove. Mumma washed the clothes by hand in a large galvanized tub with a glass washboard. The tubs sat on a long bench in the kitchen. After the wash was finished, the tubs were hung on the backside of the house and the clothes outside on a clothesline to dry. Mumma's older girls brought the dried clothes in, folded the sheets, towels and facecloths and put them away. We did very little ironing because our ironing didn't suit Mumma.

Mumma was a member of the Mount Denson Loyal Sewing Circle. The circle consisted of women who came from the surrounding community. She really enjoyed meeting and working with them at the Mount Denson community hall. During their meetings, I think these ladies took a few minutes to catch up on community news and inform each other of their children's misbehaviour. However, they certainly didn't waste their time. They sewed the most beautiful quilts you ever wished to see. There were a variety of patterns—patchwork, star, pinwheel and others. They were all very neatly hand sewn. The quilts Mumma purchased from the group looked beautiful on our beds.

Mumma had a lot of pride. She wouldn't ask for handouts. If anyone had anything to give her, such as discarded clothes, they had better offer them to her in a proper manner. If not, she refused to receive them. We often wore second-hand clothes that Mumma made look as new as possible by washing, starching and ironing them. Mumma made good use of everything. She washed and bleached the flour and sugar bags until they were white. From them, she made pillowcases and dresser runners which her girls embroidered, as well as petticoats (slips) for the girls. She was always using her Singer foot peddle sewing machine to make her girls dresses from hand-me-downs. When she had sewn, washed and starched these dresses, they looked beautiful. These were the times when people had very little compared to today. However little, it was a lot to us living in the era of the Great Depression. Mumma also told us she used to sew ticks for beds on the sewing machine. She stuffed these ticks with straw or goose feathers. Goose feathers were

plentiful in late fall when the farmers killed the geese to sell
their own use. There was a time when my older sister sle
ticks and she told me they were nice and high on the bed
were first made, but then sometimes they sank into two troughs,
leaving a ridge between the sleepers until they were re-stuffed.

Like in all the community homes, we had wooden beds in our
house and wallpaper on the walls. One time Mumma found bedbugs
in the boys' room. The minute Mumma sprayed the corner crevices of
the beds, the bed bugs came marching out like soldiers in a parade.
This Black Flag spraying process was repeated a few times, yet the
stray bugs still lingered around. Finally one day after school I found
upstairs all torn apart. There were neither beds nor mattresses in the
boys' room and the wallpaper was torn off the wall. Curious me tried
to hang around to find out what was going on. Mumma was not in a
very pleasant mood and told me to change my clothes and go outside
to play. It was outside behind the barn that I found the mattresses were
being burnt. New beds and mattresses were brought in, the walls
were re-papered and it was good-bye bed bugs.

There were some bare, board floors in the homes and the women
didn't use mops. Using a scrubbing brush they scrubbed the floor on
their knees. Mumma would put a kneeling pad under her knees. This
pad was a soft cushion that protected her knees from the hard floors.
She would scrub the bare board floor as white as snow. One place you
would find a bare, board floor was in the dairy room of large farm
houses. This was the little room on the side of a farm house where the
large milk cans, crocks, pails, butter churns, and other dairy utensils
were kept. After the farmers milked the cows, they put the pails of
milk into the dairy room. Here the women strained the milk through
a cheesecloth strainer, put it into the separating machine, then put it
into the large milk cans ready to use or sell.

During World War Two, food was on ration. Each household was
allowed a certain quantity of flour, sugar, tea, butter and other food
products considered to be diet staples for Nova Scotian families.
Ration coupons were issued for these foods. This meant that even if
you had money to buy them, you couldn't without a coupon. The

women in Mount Denson considered these ration coupons a valuable possession and therefore did not destroy any coupons they did not use. Instead, they saved coupons and exchanged them with other women, as some families used more of one thing than they did of another. Mumma made a lot of bread, as we were a large family, so she traded other coupons for flour coupons. Mumma was a beautiful bread maker and always had home-made bread in the house. It took days to make the yeast starter from potatoes and hops, so the women usually made a couple of months' supply at a time, which they stored in a cool place in tightly corked stone jars. Once in a while, when Mumma made bread, she made Daddy a breakfast of fried bread dough, which he spread with molasses and ate with a hot cup of tea. And Mumma always baked brown bread to serve with baked beans for Saturday night supper. She would often say, "Anyone coming to my house is more than welcome to have a cup of tea and I always have a piece of bread and molasses to offer them, if nothing else." Her copper tea kettle was always hissing on the stove and somehow she had more than molasses to serve with bread and tea. It might have been stewed rhubarb, strawberries and cream in season, or apple sauce, which was plentiful anytime.

There were eleven children in my family. It was like two families in one to me. The first family included my older brothers and sisters, Reginald, Ruth, Ruby, William Harrison, and Charles, whom I cannot remember playing with as a child. Next came Arthur, then me, followed by Mona, Regina, Alonzo and Byron. Since I fit in the middle, the seventh child, I felt that from Arthur down we were the second family. I don't know if any of my older brothers or sisters were born at home or not. I do know that a doctor was in attendance for all of Mumma's deliveries, including mine.

It was a beautiful day in the Annapolis Valley, so they tell me, on the day I was born. The tidewater breeze off the Avon River filled the air with the smell of apple blossoms. Fruit trees were all abloom and tulips were opening their petals. Lovely bell-shaped, white flowers of the lilies were appearing. The farmers in the fields were sowing seeds and fishermen were hooking trout from Black Brook.

invisible shadows

Being an offspring of such a blood mix I'm sure I caused the attending doctor and nurse some questions about which "race" box to check on their forms. They probably said, "Let's see, Negro, native, white, or pencil 'mulatto' into the margin." Was I a misfit from birth or just another child stepping out into some unknown destiny? Born so small into a world of such unknown destiny it is little wonder Daddy dropped the "des" from destiny and nicknamed me "Tiny."

When I was only a few days old, a native lady from Shubenacadie came to our house selling baskets. Seeing me in Mumma's arms, she told Mumma I resembled a little papoose and asked what my name was. Since Mumma had not yet named me, the lady asked Mumma to give me her native name, Ferne. Sure enough, Mumma gave me the name and on June 26, 1935 I was registered Ferne Irene States. Strange as it may be, while I was still being called Tiny, Verna, a white neighbour in the community, was talking with Mumma and she asked her my name. When told it was Ferne, Verna told Mumma, "Ferne is not a name. Change it to Verna after me." Would you know that from that day on I was called Verna? I'm not sure why, but I was never told the story about my name while growing up. It wasn't until 1967, when John and I were taking our first trip to the USA and I needed my birth certificate, that I was made aware of this. Although my name was Verna, I was still registered as Ferne. I was told the story about my name when I brought this to Mumma's attention. I had to go through the red tape of having my name changed from Ferne to Verna. Yet, to this day my native resemblance and peculiar inner feeling give me the sense that I am still Ferne. I was the kind of creature the world wasn't ready for: the seventh child, the uneven number, the one the family referred to as odd and contrary. Family members were quiet, easygoing, passive, stay-at-home people and quite happy in life's situation. Me, you always knew when I was around. I had to know what was happening around me. Life was an open door and my curiosity guided me through.

During the 1940s, when World War Two was going on, people were mostly optimistic about the outcome. During those days, people didn't carry placards and hold demonstrations to express their political views. They used other forms of expression to make a political statement, such as Daddy did when he wrote the poem "V for Victory," which was published in the *Hants Journal*, our local newspaper:

Victory

V- stands for Victory

I - stands for Islands, no enemy can take

C- stands for Courage, they never can break

T- stands for Tough luck, they've already had. But they'll never give up, let it be ever so bad.

O- stands for Ocean, where the high billows roll, but the ships of Great Britain have it under control

R- stands for Roosevelt, who has proved to be true, and stands beside England and seen the thing through

Y- stands for Yonder, where the bombers will roar, till we beat all enemies, as we have done before.

Daddy never saw himself as a poet or historian; he never wrote a book nor compiled any history. Yet the conversations we shared, the stories of life he told and the examples he set is history in every sense of the word. Sometimes when he was telling a story about his life in the valley he would put it into poetry. Oh, how I wish I had written some of these poems in my notes. Daddy loved his valley roots; farming and tilling the land made him feel happy. I hold the same love for my valley roots as Daddy did and, like Mumma, I say what I mean and I mean what I say.

I was a very slim, light-skinned child with two long black braids down my back. Each braid had a ribbon tied at the end. Mumma put my hair in ringlets for Sunday School and special occasions. All during my school days, I never had an argument or fight with anyone. I wanted to be everyone's friend. Whenever I got the feeling someone didn't want to play with me, I went off by myself and had a little cry and told myself I wouldn't play with that person even if he/she wanted to play with me.

One of my favourite childhood memories is of spending time with Aunt Eva. Knowing that I was one of her favourites, Aunt Eva's love

invisible shadows

and attention made me feel very special. She was always happy and didn't mind me pestering her with questions as I rubbed liniment on her swollen ankles. Being the inquisitive child I was, I was always seeking answers to my questions—Why do I have to be inoculated? Why can't I play with Billy? and How come I can't sleep over at Mary's house? Mumma didn't like to answer a lot of my questions so she often pretended to be too busy to do so. Like Mumma I often pretended too. I pretended I had forgotten that I was asking her the same questions I had asked her a few days ago. Mumma would get fed up with my questions and tell me to go play. Play to me was taking a walk with friends along the pasture path, gathering chestnuts to make pipes and miniature carts and such. Or drawing hopscotch squares in the backyard with my friends or playing games like red light and send rover

Aunt Eva, hanging clothes on the clothesline, ca. 1949. She used to catch rain water in big wooden barrels for washing clothes and for other household chores. She was an extraordinary person, like a grandmother and a big sister both.

over. At times, I could be stubborn, like Daddy, if I didn't get my own way and I would go off by myself. But my all alone times were great. I would think about how famous I was going to be someday living in a huge castle by the sea. Sometimes I would daydream about the adventures I would like to take riding up high mountains on a motorcycle or writing a poem about something on my mind. The strangest thing I did when alone was create mathematical formulas with my birth date. I was born the thirtieth day of the fifth month, on the fifth day of the week in the year 1935 and I was my parents' seventh child. I discovered you could add, subtract, multiply and divide these numbers to come up with the same numbers. The day plus the month equals the year—thirty plus five equals thirty-five. The year minus the month equals the day—thirty-five minus five equals thirty. The day of the

Mount Denson homestead, with the huge elm tree by the driveway, ca. 1970. Our house was one of the first in Mount Denson to have a television; when I went home there was always a group of young people gathered around it in the living room.

invisible shadows

week multiplied by my place in the family equals the year I was born—five times seven equals thirty-five. The year divided by the day of the week equals my place in the family—thirty-five divided by five equals seven. Perhaps now you can understand why the family referred to me as odd!

Our family home was a two-storey house with three bedrooms. The bedrooms were upstairs and on the main floor were our kitchen, dining room and living room. We also had a cellar for storing vegetables, fruit and preserves. My parents had the house built after they were married, while they were living in the big old house down by the railroad tracks. At the top of the stairs was the boys' room with a double and single bed where Alonzo, Harrison, and Byron slept. Next was the girls' room. There was a double and single bed in our room. Mona had the single bed and Regina and I shared the double bed. Daddy and Mumma had their bedroom down the hall.

In spite of money problems brought on by the war, home improvements began, made possible because Daddy compensated his earnings by stoning up wells and carving wooden axe handles and ladders to sell. Mumma also took part-time work as a cook at Harvie's Boarding House, just up the road from home. The changes in our house began during one particular spring cleaning when I was eight. Mumma got pretty, bright wallpaper and floor linoleum from Simpson's and Eaton's mail order department stores. My older sister helped her put the new wallpaper on the walls with flour and water paste. Daddy and Mamma covered all the floors with linoleum. Mumma put a new piece of oilcloth on the table and when she cleaned the stove all shiny with black lead polish, in came our new refrigerator. We were delighted to have this new appliance so we could freeze our berry juice.

Soon after, the peddle sewing machine was replaced with an electric one and wash day became easier with the wringer washer. The wringer washer changed the way we played after school. When we got the wringer washer, the long wash bench that Mumma used to place against the kitchen wall to put her wash tubs on was no longer needed. Therefore, she no longer moved the chairs out from the wall to make room for the bench. We used to come home from school to line up the chairs to make a train or a bus. The child sitting in the front chair was the driver.

Changes were coming rapidly but some things remained the same during our home-improvement days. Our bath water was always shared. Saturday night used to be bath night and we used to take turns getting into the big wash tub of warm water on the kitchen floor by the oven door. It was usually late evening and the kitchen door was locked. If anyone came home or to visit, they had to go to the front door. In summer, our hair used to be shampooed outside on the back doorstep and we sat under the big elm tree on a quilt until our hair dried. There we played with our dolls or read a book. Books weren't plentiful, which meant we often read the same book a couple of times and of course we shared them with each other.

Although we did like to share things with each other, there was a time when I was not so happy to do this. My future brother-in-law, who was stationed away with the Armed Forces, mailed me a parcel of chocolate bars, gum and peanuts. This was the first parcel I ever received through the mail in my whole life and at the age of eight I didn't want to share any of my candy with anyone. Of course, this was unthinkable to Mumma and, like it or not, I was made to share the contents of my parcel.

Suppertime was the time when the family was all together. The dining room table was kept covered with an oilcloth table cloth. Every suppertime this table was fully set by my sister Mona or I. Sometimes I became frustrated with setting the table because Mumma wanted the knives and forks and spoons in their proper place, and the cream and sugar dish had to be "just so" in the centre of the table. We all ate supper together with Mumma jumping up and down to serve us. This was our big meal of the day. After supper, Mona and I washed and dried the dishes. Regina didn't. As the youngest she never had any responsibilities. Before bedtime we had a cup of milk and a piece of bread.

Every night we were in bed by eight o'clock. We'd get down on our knees by our beds and pray, "Now I lay me down to sleep, I pray the Lord my soul to Keep. If I die before I wake, I Pray the Lord my

invisible shadows

soul to take. God bless Mumma and Daddy." Then every night my sisters and I would tell stories or sing ourselves to sleep. Sometimes I'd change my voice to tell a scary story and scare the daylights out of Mona and Regina. After this they would stop talking and I would turn out the light. I never knew if they were sleeping or just too scared to say anything.

To celebrate our birthdays, we never had a birthday cake or a party, but we always got a special birthday gift. On my fourteenth birthday I got a bicycle and I still have the baby brownie camera I got on my fifteen birthday. My first real gold jewellery I received on my sixteenth birthday—an identification bracelet and birthstone ring with my initials on it, which I still have to this day too.

Although we lived in a white neighbourhood, our mother had a way of providing us with black cultural ties that we needed to affirm our racial identity. One of the annual events we looked forward to was the Windsor Plains Coloured Sunday School Picnic at Evangeline Beach in July. Here we got to meet some of our relatives and play with some of our cousins from Windsor Plains. The day of the picnic, a couple of big trucks stopped at the Shore Road corner to pick us up. Even when we didn't attend the picnic, we waved to the truck loads of people as they passed our corner on their way to Evangeline Beach. When we attended the picnic, we were up at dawn, swallowed breakfast in a hurry because we were too excited to eat. While Mumma packed the picnic baskets, we were getting dressed to await the 8 a.m. arrival of the truckloads of people. We sat on benches on the open back of the truck with the wind blowing through our hair as we sang such songs as "Shoo Fly Pie," "She'll be coming Around the Mountain When She Comes," and "When the Moon Shines Over the Cowshed." We spent all day swimming, playing games and eating. Everyone brought food. We made good of this day because as children we didn't get to visit our relatives from the Plains and only saw them occasionally when they visited our house.

Winters were long and cold with a lot of snow. I can't remember a single Christmas without snow when I was a child. During the Christmas holidays we loved to see falling snow. We children went outside in the snowstorms to sing all the Christmas carols: "It Came Upon the Midnight Clear," "Hark the Herald Angels Sing," "Away in a Manger," "Star of the East," "The First Noel," "Silent Night" and "O Come All Ye Faithful." If Christmas was on a Sunday, we went to Sunday School. We learned at a very young age the true story of Christmas as told in St. Luke, Chapter 2. Daddy went into the woods and cut a real live Christmas tree with bushy branches. We helped trim the tree with glass bulbs, lights, icicles and home-made popcorn chains. We didn't have any outdoor Christmas lights or decorations.

We didn't have TV and shopping malls, so we only saw Santa Claus in the Eaton's and Simpson's catalogues. A lot of our toys—our doll cradle and highchair, for example—were handmade and Mumma sewed an outfit for our doll. The boys' sleds and hockey sticks were handmade. Christmas Eve we left a plate of cookies and glass of milk out for Santa Claus and a carrot for his reindeer. We hung our stocking behind the kitchen stove before we went to bed. On Christmas morning, we found our stocking filled with nuts, candy, a big toy candy on top and an orange in the toe. I really believed Santa Claus left my toys and filled my stocking on Christmas Eve. Every Christmas morning, we had home-made doughnuts. I still make home-made doughnuts and eggnog on Christmas morning to keep this tradition going. We had turkey dinner with cranberry sauce and mincemeat pie for dessert. At about six o'clock, Mumma cut a huge tray of different kinds of Christmas cakes and loaves and made a pot of Christmas syrup.

Though my parents worked extremely hard, they could only provide the same for their family as any average family in the community could. We certainly never became the richest family in our community, but never the poorest either. Ours was a life limited to the necessities. From the outside, our home was nothing more than a simple structure, but the inside housed a hard-working father with a stubborn sense of fairness, a strong-willed and caring mother and their children. This was a home where love was rarely preached but constantly practised, and where discipline was a part of everyday life.

I grew up at a time when parents held themselves responsible for their children's behaviour. Fathers guided and provided for their families. Women accepted that their highest calling was as mother and housekeeper. Mumma ran a tight ship at our house and her authority continued right into adulthood. Her belief that children were to be seen and not heard led her to set strict rules that the children could not question but only abide by.

The standards for our behaviour were very strict. The most common instrument used in disciplining us was the switch—a long, thin twig that was sometimes stripped of its leaves. When we were forbidden to do something, we rarely if ever disobeyed. Knowing we were only given one verbal warning, we knew that if we would receive a spanking. The third time it was a whipping.

Daddy let Mumma dish out the discipline in our family. It was not her belief to "spare the rod and spoil the child." When we needed the switch, we got it and we got it good. One of my brothers often did the very things he knew we were not allowed to do. When he got caught, it meant a switching. As mother tingled his legs with a switch she would say, "You may be hard headed boy but I will either make you or break you." It was this form of an upbringing that instilled in me a certain respect for authority—something solid I carried out into society as I became an adult.

The older children helped in gathering the eggs and doing other chores. Chores gave us a sense of responsibility. Back in the 1930s and 40s when homes didn't have any inside plumbing, we emptied and cleaned the chamber pails before leaving for school in the morning. On the way home for lunch we picked up the family mail from the post office and after school we ran errands at Ainsley MacDonald's grocery store. We went next door to Cecil MacDonald's candy factory where we could get broken pieces of candy for a penny or two. Whenever Ainsley's daughter Julia served me at the store, I was on my best behaviour because Julia was my Sunday school teacher.

Some days we were sent off to Hantsport to L. B. Harvie grocery store. We liked to go to Hantsport on errands. Sometimes we crossed the aboiteau over a plank bridge (which washed out in 1971), took our shoes off, sat on a plank and put our feet in the water. In cold weather, we threw stones into the water. After we crossed the aboiteau, we walked out to the railroad track, past the York Theatre, into Hantsport. Other times, we took the main highway over the bridge, past the high granite monument of William Hall. Having read about and also heard stories from my Daddy about this brave and adventurous man, I often stopped on the way to Hantsport and gazed at his monument. Sometimes the thought crossed my mind that I would like to do something great to earn such a monument.

William Hall was the son of an escaped slave from Virginia who came to Nova Scotia on a British warship around 1812. William was born April 28, 1827 in Horton, Kings County, Nova Scotia. His home was on a hill near the site of Horton Bluff Lighthouse. From the top of this hill he could view the Avon River, Avonport and Grand Pré. He began his sea life as a merchant seaman in the year 1845 and on February 2, 1852 joined the British Navy. In the summer of 1857, he was one of 410 seamen on the ship Shannon sent to Calcutta, India.

During the Indian mutiny battle at Lucknow on November 16, 1857, the order was given to attack the massive masonry walls of the Shah Nujeef, a Mohammedan temple—a virtual suicide mission. When all the crew except Hall and badly wounded lieutenant Thomas Jamie Young were killed, Hall kept loading and firing the gun until he breached the wall for the relieving forces to join the defenders. It was this noble work that earned William Hall the Victoria Cross. He was the third Canadian, the first black person and the first member of the navy to be decorated with this award. William Hall died at home in Avonport on August 25, 1904 and was buried without honours in Stony Hill graveyard, Lockhartville, leaving behind his two sisters, Mary Hall and Rachael Robinson. Needing money to pay off a debt, they put the Victorian Cross and some of William's other medals up for sale. The Nova Scotian Historical Society failed to buy these medals and they were sent to London, England. We children always entered the town of Hantsport on the corner of Main and Willet streets. It was there, in 1945, that the William Hall V. C. Branch of Halifax, the Hants County Branch and other Canadian legions purchased a plot of ground, re-buried William Hall's remains, and erected the William Hall Memorial Monument in his honour.

invisible shadows

On our way to Hantsport we always stopped at Grammy Becky's house to see if she needed an errand done. A small, neatly dressed lady who always wore a couple of dresses at a time, a long white petticoat, a shawl over her coat and a cap on her head, Grammy Becky was my great-grandmother on my mother's side. She walked into Hantsport by herself every day during the summer and a great many days in winter, yet our parents did not allow us to pass her door without checking her needs. Most times Grammy took us children in and set us up to her table for a bowl of her beautiful rabbit stew and a huge piece of apple pie and milk or one of her delicious molasses cookie-cakes. She would put some into a bag for us to take home to Daddy to have with his tea. Sometimes she gave us a lovely piece of johnny-cake with molasses and a cup of molasses tea. There were times when Grammy Becky didn't want to be troubled by anyone, let alone children. Oddly enough we knew when these times were. It was a joy to knock on her door and hear her say, "Mercy sakes child! Come right in here, set to the table and wodge your belly." We knew on those days that she didn't want to be alone. But when we knocked and she gave

Grammy Becky, ca. 1930. Sometimes we caught her sitting in her rocking chair having a smoke. She put her corncob pipe on the window ledge next to her tobacco pouch before answering the door.

us a cookie at the door and said, "Mercy sakes child! Fan along home, I know your mother wants you," we knew to leave and let her be.

When I was five or six years old, my oldest sister, Ruth, would take me to Gramma Becky's in the early evening hour. I liked to go to her house to see her beautiful display of porcelain dolls. The biggest delight of all was when she wound up her black wooden dancing dolls and let them dance or play music for us. She had several black dancing dolls and she always got a great laugh from watching them dance. What I wouldn't give to be able to visit Grammy Becky's little home in Mount Denson and see her sitting in her rocking chair by the window, with the pretty, hooked mats on her floor, the table of dolls and the many pictures that hung on her walls. I can see her now, wrapped in a shawl and wearing her big apron. Many people used to visit her for the ostensible purpose of having her "read the teacups," but mostly it was to hear her interesting talk of the old days. They enjoyed her friendly and wise sayings. Whenever Grammy Becky was asked, "how do you feel" her answer was, "Mercy-sakes child! Other than a little touch of rheumatism that steals into my joints once in a while, I am as fit as a fiddle and can still step [dance] a clog."

Of all the errands we had to run, the greatest pleasure came when we had to go to Aunt Edith's. There were two ways we could get to her house. The long way was to go right out the Apple Tree Road to the last house by the railroad track. The other way, which was much quicker, was to walk out by the railroad track. Whenever we took the track, we would stop at the Mount Denson Train Station and set around the station for a while pretending to be waiting for a train. This was a little flag station where passengers put the flag out if they wanted the train to stop. Because the bus passed by our house, we very rarely used the train, so it was a treat to hang around the station once in a while.

Whatever way we took we were glad to get there. Uncle Bill was Mi'kmaq and he could charm a bird to set on his shoulder or eat from his hand. He travelled by horse and wagon. His horse's name was Queenie. Sometimes if Uncle Bill was late coming home and too tired to drive, he would lay in the back of his wagon and say "go home

Queenie," and the horse would take him home. As a child, I thought Uncle Bill was a magician because he could charm the animals.

In the 1930s and 40s, just about every farm house in the community had a couch in the kitchen. During the winter there was a line above the stove used to finish drying damp clothes taken off the outdoor clothesline. Also, when we came into the house with our mitts soaked from rolling snowballs, buildings snow forts and breaking icicles off the eaves of the house and eating them like frozen Popsicles, we hung our mitts on the line to dry for our next outing. During the evening the man of the house was usually found lying on the couch, smoking his pipe. Daddy smoked Old Chum pipe tobacco and White Owl cigars and chewed Club chewing tobacco. There always was a good fire burning in the stove. Some wood was put in the oven for drying and the oven door was left open for the warm air to escape. We'd pull a chair up to the oven door, stick our feet in on the wood and sit around the stove inhaling the sweet smell of wood burning, eating apples, talking about our day and just enjoying the cozy feeling of home and neighbours.

There were no mansions in our community but the homes were filled with the warmth of community love. There weren't any "welcome mats" at our doors, yet everyone who entered was welcome. Ma Harris, a white neighbour, would sometimes drop-in for a cup of tea with Mumma in the morning and often came to play a game of cards to pass the early evening when Daddy was working the four to twelve shift. Another white friend, Jean Wile, frequently dropped in to sample a quick taste of whatever Mumma was cooking for dinner. She just loved Mumma's cooking. Mumma always knew when she saw Jean coming over the hill that she would be stopping in for a sample.

Some of my happiest moments were when the bus stopped at the corner of Shore Road and Aunt Eva got off. We would immediately forget about what we were doing at the time and rush off to meet her. The picture of the broad smile on her face when she saw us running to greet her is still clear in my mind today. She was always so happy and jolly, a pleasure to be around. When Daddy and Mumma were at work, Aunt Eva would put a record on the record player and dance around the living room floor with us. She could step dance real good and could belt out some great tunes on her harmonica. One of our favourites was "Polly Wolly Doodle." Get togethers at our house were few, but once-in-a-while, on special occasions, a few people gathered at our house to play music, sing and dance. While Mumma was in the dining room preparing refreshments, we sneaked down the steps far enough to peer through the stair rails at the dancers in the living room. If Aunt Eva saw us, she came, took us down to the corner of the hall and had a quick dance around with us before Mumma could catch us out of bed.

Papa (Mumma's father) was another visitor we liked to see. Whenever the Nova Scotia Power crew was working in Mount Denson, Papa came to our house for lunch and never left without giving us children a penny or two. When Papa visited us on a Sunday he was always well dressed in a suit, with a felt hat and spats on his shoes. He wore a long gold watch chain that hung from his vest pocket. I felt Papa was fit to be a king, always so kind and gentle.

Some evenings relatives and friends came by our home after a long hard day of work and joined in those "sit-around the stove" times and told stories. Good storytellers and singers were great assets, as there were no televisions. Sometimes the stories were about personal experiences or sometimes they were about the big fish that got away, the heavy bags of potatoes or flour one could carry on his back, the coldest winter, or how far out to sea one could swim.

I remember one story about a bitter, cold winter day when a farmer called his pigs so that he could feed them. It was so cold that the freezing air froze his words, and the pigs didn't hear his call. They didn't arrive home to be fed until the farmer's words thawed out in the spring. Another story was about a young girl who became pregnant. Her father accused the neighbour's son and the young lad was taken to court for the wrong he had done. After the lad told the court his side of the story, the young girl was called to the stand. She was asked, "Do you swear to tell the truth, the whole truth and nothing but the truth, so help you God?" "Yes." She answered. The judge then asked her, "Who is the father of your expected child?" She answered, "Your honour, it's like this. If you lay a log of wood across a sawhorse and cut it with a crosscut saw, how would you know which tooth cut?" The young man got off. End of case.

These were good tales, but the best and funniest stories were told by two of Mumma's sisters. One such story told to us was about a woman who stole a dress from a store in Windsor. One day a store owner told my aunt that a woman had stolen a dress from her store; she described the woman and asked my aunt if she knew her, which she did. The next time the woman went into the store, the owner confronted her about taking the dress. The woman knew who had told on her and when she saw my aunt she asked her why she had told. My aunt berated her, saying that she should not be stealing and that this was something she herself would never do. The woman became angry and told my aunt in an indignant voice that she was the one who stole things. My aunt said she had never stolen a thing in her life. The woman called her a liar and repeated that all she ever did was steal—other women's men. Without losing a beat, my aunt said she stood guilty as accused.

Many times my other aunt told the story, "Don't Touch the Family Tree." She told us the family tree was made up of members of various skin tones, ranging from very dark to white. She said the reason for this was when the old folks lived on the plantations in the United States, the masters put the black men in harnesses and used them to plough the fields like horses. While the men were ploughing the fields, the masters visited the huts where their workers' wives were. So, we all got mixed up like a dog's breakfast and when the *Mayflower* was pulling out from shore, we jumped on and came to Canada with the rest of them. Now, that's the way my aunt told the story.

Downhill from the corner of the Shore Road where we lived there was a hollow. After the hollow there was a big hill, then the flats to the railroad track. The last house over the track on Shore Road belonged to Captain Billy MacKinlay, a sea captain. Here there were ruins of the MacKinlay's old shipyard and bordering his property was the Avon River. As children we were forbidden to play around the shipyard. Be that as it may, when nobody was in sight, we played for ever so long around the hulls of those old abandoned ships. We pretended to be sea captains and sailors sailing out to sea. Sometimes we were Columbus and his crew members naming the ships the *Nina*, *Pinta* and *Santa Maria*. Sometimes we pretended to be Long John Silver and the pirates.

Certain times as I played around these old abandoned ships, I wondered if any of them had carried my ancestors to this land. I had sometimes heard my aunt say, "we came over on the *Mayflower* with the rest of them." Of course, Captain MacKinlay's ships hadn't even been built when my ancestors would have come over years before; however, as a child, these bits of information made me curious.

Of course it wasn't true, but Joe told me that the *Mayflower* was a slave ship. Joe was an African who came to Hantsport on one of the ships coming into port for a load of gypsum. He jumped ship while in Hantsport and Uncle Andrew took him in. While staying with Uncle Andrew, Joe told us children that slave ships brought our black ancestors to Canada. He was talking about a ship that carried free slaves from America to Canada (probably a British warship). We children didn't know if Joe was telling us the truth or a fairy tale. Many things Joe said we could not understand because of his heavy accent. When Joe came to our house for tea, he often told my mother stories about life in Africa and the food they ate.

One day Joe made peanut soup for Uncle Andrew's supper. Nobody on the Shore Road had heard of peanut soup, so we thought that Uncle Andrew would get sick. Instead, Uncle Andrew said the peanut soup was very good. About a year after Joe came to stay with Uncle Andrew, he went to Windsor and nobody heard from him again. Some people believed he was picked up by the authorities for being in Canada illegally. Joe had piqued my curiosity about my ancestors and I always wondered if what he had said was true. As a child I pieced together what little I could from the different things the adults said. However, it wasn't until years later when I began researching black history, that I learned that one of the greatest influxes of Blacks to Nova Scotia came following the War of 1812. By 1815 about three thousand Blacks lived in Nova Scotia. I found records in Grammy's family bible that show that somewhere below the deck of one of those free slave ships, my ancestors were being carried to freedom in a new land.

Mount Denson was a close-knit community of kind, hard-working farmers. Sharing was a way of life. We knew we were black, but our colour did not prevent us from benefiting from the warmth of our community. We were just a well-respected community family like any other. This fact was never more evident than when tragedy struck our family. It was August 3, 1940 on a Saturday evening. Daddy was working the four to midnight shift. Mumma was in Windsor shopping. My sister Ruby and my brother Charlie were doing an errand at the store for my uncle. On their way back home, just a short distance from the store, my brother was hit by a car, thrown into the ditch and left there. The driver did not stop. I remember Ruby running into the house crying and screaming, "Someone killed Charlie." Everyone in our house was crying when Grammy Affie and Aunt Eunice arrived. I was only five. When Mumma's two sisters, Aunt Dot and Aunt Annie, came, they took us upstairs. The next day Grammy Affie told us we would not be able to play with Charlie anymore, because he was sleeping in his coffin in her living room and he would be going to live with the Lord. We were kept upstairs and we never saw Charlie again. I only remember a long black car driving slowly into Grampy and Grammy's yard and my sister Ruth yelling at us to come away from the window. I also heard someone crying downstairs and I couldn't make sense of what was happening.

After the funeral was over, I overheard Daddy and Mumma and Grampy Charlie on the back stoop talking about what had happened. Some neighbourhood men setting on the store stoop had heard the bang, investigated it and called the police. This quick action on their part enabled the police to apprehend the drunken hit-and-run driver just a few miles on the other side of Hantsport. The driver was charged with manslaughter, tried in a Windsor court and sentenced to a short time in jail. It was the feeling of many community neighbours that the driver should have receiver a harsher sentence. Community friends and neighbours joined family members in Grammy's parlour where my brother was laid out. Neighbours brought food as was the custom when death came to our community. Although this was a sad time for the family, the consolation we received from the whole community was overwhelming and comforting.

Although we all had chores to do, at the age of five, when we were still knee-high to a grasshopper, our most important responsibility became school. Mount Denson School was about a mile from our house and we had to walk to and from school each day. This two-room schoolhouse, with a huge wood-coal stove in the centre of each of the primary and advanced rooms, opened the door to basic education. We sat in desks that were lined-up in rows according to grades. Each desk had an inkwell with indelible ink in it. Each morning, class began with the singing of "O Canada!" followed by the "Lord's Prayer"; we sang "God Save Our King" in the afternoon. Time periods were allotted for each subject: arithmetic, reading, spelling, English, history and geography. We had two outhouses, one for the girls and one for the boys.

The classroom was a place where we learnt to get along like a family. It was this sort of atmosphere that gave me the feeling of being at one with my white classmates and school friends. Oh, we sometimes had arguments and disagreements, but there was never any racial tension or conflict between students. In home economics class the girls could knit a hat and scarf set, or sew a skirt. One sewing class in particular stands out in my mind. Mumma bought a pretty print cotton of white background with bright red strawberries on it. My love for this piece of material caused me to put my best effort into making a beautiful skirt. Having grown up in a time when practical mothers considered sewing and housekeeping essential to their daughters' education, Mumma was well pleased with the work I put into my skirt. I was proud to wear it to school.

Students were given homework, and at home after supper it was study and homework time. If we didn't have our homework completed or know our lessons, we could be sure we would have to remain after school the next day. Some nights I studied so hard that when I went to bed the lesson was so strong in my mind I couldn't even hear the rumbling of "The Midnight Special" coming down the track.

Teachers took an interest in their students and discipline was very much a part of learning. The teacher often had a pointer in her hand as she walked around the classroom viewing the students' work. If she caught us daydreaming, we got our knuckles cracked with the pointer, or worse, she used the leather strap. Every Friday was a review of the week's work to help us prepare for the major examinations.

But school wasn't all work; we had extra curricular activities, which I participated in wholeheartedly. Like many other schools in those days, ours had a Junior Red Cross Group, which gave us first-hand knowledge of organization and participation. As a girl, I just couldn't wait for Friday afternoon's Red Cross meeting. We elected our class president, secretary and treasurer, who took their places at the front of the class room for each meeting. The president called the meeting to order, the secretary called the roll and read the minutes

Mount Denson School, ca. 1948. I got along well with my white schoolmates at this mixed school, where I gained the self-confidence I needed to understand that accomplishments had no colour.

Mount Denson

and the treasurer gave the financial report. Each student paid their five cents dues, some of which went to the Canadian Red Cross Society. We Red Cross students knit facecloths from white twine to put into the soldiers' care packages to be shipped overseas during the war. Although we had no uniform, all the students had a Red Cross Pin purchased from the dues money. We wore our pins with great pride as they indicated we were members of a special group practising the principles of community service.

Canadian Girls in Training (CGIT) was another group worthy of being a member of. Its official uniform, a white middy blouse and a navy skirt, gave us a sense of pride and respect for ourselves and our group. We had one meeting a month conducted by an adult leader, who talked to us about how good citizens behaved. Each month one of the girls would do an inspection to make sure our nails were clean and our uniforms were neat and tidy.

Me, second row, fourth from left, in home economics class, ca. 1948. My classmates and I model the skirts we made. I won prize ribbons at the Windsor Exhibition for my knitted scarf and tea biscuits.

invisible shadows

Our school participated in the Hants County Music Festivals and, somehow, the music teacher had me singing in these festivals. I had no interest in singing because I felt I didn't do it well, but the teacher convinced me that I had an alto voice much needed in our choir. She couldn't have realized at the time that it would have taken more than a miracle to make a singer out of me. The first Hants County Music Festival was held at the Hantsport York Theatre on May 19, 1944. Our music teacher had us practising over and over again the songs we were going to sing in the musical festival. We practised these songs so much that some nights I sang them in my sleep. On the day of the festival, the kids were all dressed-up. I wore my Sunday school clothes: black patent leather shoes polished to a shine, white ankle socks and my Sunday school dress (which was factory-made and ordered from a mail order store). I was as proud as a peacock when I got dressed in my Sunday best. Our teacher was very proud of us too on these special occasions.

Another school event was our school Christmas concert. We always had a Christmas pageant with a manger, three kings and angels. The manger was made of fir or spruce boughs and one of the girls brought in a doll and doll cradle from home. The parts of the kings were played by three boys dressed in bathrobes and bandannas with gifts in their hands to represent gold, frankincense and myrrh, while the girls had halos and dressed in white dresses made from crepe paper. A narrator read the story of Jesus's birth while the angels sang Christmas carols. After the pageant was over, Santa Claus came and passed out a gift and treat to each child. The gifts were made possible through the exchange of names between classmates.

Our school days were much more than the classroom and school programs. Students played together, walked together, studied together and had all kinds of adventures together. There weren't any school buses and we came home for lunch, so we did a lot of walking. Six or seven of us walked to and from school together, and sometimes we stopped at Macdonald Store to get some candy for recess. For a nickel we got a big chocolate bar or a big bag of mixed penny candy. We could get two honeymoons for a cent, five licorice mice for a cent and a variety of other candy for a cent. We liked to top our candy bag off with a delicious queen's lunch, which was about two inches square, filled with coconut, caramel and covered with chocolate. Jerusalem Choices, with its coconut mixture centre and taffy like-covering, was also a favourite. It was great to have just a penny to stop at the store to buy candy for recess. We sometimes bought different candy and traded with each other—one honeymoon went for three licorice mice.

Our school break-time (recess and lunch) was spent playing games like baseball. Two kids were captains and each one took a turn at picking another kid to be on his or her team. When all the kids were chosen, the game began. One team was up for batting the rubber ball, and the other team chose a pitcher and a catcher. We had two bats: a real round bat for the boys and a flat, home-made bat for the girls. The bases were simply large rocks placed in the field to mark first, second and third base, and home plate. The girls played outfield and had a turn at bat. The first, second and third basemen were boys; they used their baseball gloves to catch the ball. It was a great honour the day the girls were promoted to play second base! We played other games too, like tag, red light and hide and seek, during good weather. We also enjoyed hiking and climbing trees.

We knew the warm season was ending when the days got shorter and the breeze off of the Avon River got cooler. The harvest was gathered from the fields and fruit picked from the trees and vines. The women prepared fruit and vegetables for winter—bottles and bottles of pickles, relish and chow-chow. Farmers built their homes with cellars under them, without full foundations like today. Cellars stored the winter's supply of food. The home-made pickles and preserves were kept on shelves; vegetables were kept in bins of sand or sawdust; and salt meat, fish and apples were kept in apple barrels. Sauerkraut and cider were stored in cider kegs, which were smaller than the barrels. In the late fall men used to bank the homes with sawdust to keep the winter draft out.

Each fall three or four men took their steer or pig to a certain farmer's barnyard for killing. The farmer had a huge outside fire with tin barrels of boiling water on it to be used for the slaughtering. They built a large hanging frame to hang the animal up for scraping. The slaughtered animal hung there overnight. When our pig arrived back home, it was in the form of roast pork, bacon, ham and other pieces that were pickled in a barrel of salt brine. Daddy gave us girls the pig tails and we baked them in the oven. Often they came out so hard we could barely eat them, yet we thought they were fit for a queen simply because we had prepared them ourselves.

Fall came to a close on October 31, "Halloween." We celebrated this day with a school party, bobbing for apples, dressing-up in a costume and mask and going door-to-door trick or treating. Usually we got enough treats to last us until just about Christmas. We anxiously awaited winter so we could go coasting off Dickie's Hill or down the Shore Road. During the long, bitter cold winter evenings we enjoyed the coast from the corner of the road to the hollow on our sleds. We didn't have to worry about being interrupted by a car coming up or down the road, because in the 1940s and 50s, cars were a rarity.

One winter, my brother Chum took two sleds, put one in front and one in back, nailed a wide piece of board on them and made a bobsled that held four or five of us. Chum's bobsled was the fastest on the road. The person sitting up front had the duty of steering. The last person to get on would give a big push, jump on and off we would go, holding on for dear life so we didn't fall off and upset the sled before we reached the hollow. This made for a very thrilling ride down the hill in the snow.

We also built snow forts along the side of the road. Three or four of us would build a snow fort a short distance from the next group of kids. There were always at least four forts in close range. Once the forts were up, we put piles of snowballs in them, preparing ourselves for the game of war. When everyone was ready, we went to battle with our enemies. When all the snowballs in one fort were used up, the kids in that fort moved to the fort of their choice. This went on until all but one fort would be out of snowballs. That fort was declared the winning army.

We also played on the frozen ponds. The girls skated at one end of the pond, while the boys used the other end for hockey. In those days women and girls didn't wear slacks—we wore dresses or skirts, even in winter. Consequently, when going out into the open air, our knees would often just about freeze. Girls wore long beige cotton stockings and heavy wool knee-highs over them. I never liked those long cotton stockings when I became a teenager. Every time I went skating I took the stockings off and left just my knee-highs on. We sat on a snow bank to put our skates on and skated for hours in a skirt. After skating we sat on the snow bank again, took our skates off and walked home half frozen. Once my brother tried to teach me how to skate backwards on one foot like Barbara Ann Scott. I fell and hit my head so hard on the ice I could smell my brains. There were many big ponds to go ice skating on. We had such happy times—no fighting or quarrelling, no liquor or smoking other than a couple of teen-age boys. Sometimes during skating time someone made a big bonfire where we could take time out to get warm. Sometimes we went skiing. Our skis just had straps that went around our feet. Some kids had poles, but those that didn't could get along without them. We'd climb up the hill and ski down. Often on our way home we dropped in at one of our friends' homes and their mother would have a big pot of hot chocolate ready for us.

In the spring, the boys made go-carts from old wagon wheels and wide boards. They started at the corner of Shore Road and drove down to the hollow. From there they pulled the carts up the big hill and drove down to the railroad track before they went back to the corner for another trip down the road. The girls took our doll and doll carriage for a walk down the road over the big hill and close enough to the railway track to wave to the passengers on the train.

Sometimes early on a Sunday morning, Daddy would take us for a walk out to the Jud Spring, just to get a drink of spring water. Sometimes he would take tin cans with wire handles with him and hang them on maple trees. We used to stand and watch the sap dripping into the cans. A few days later when he brought the cans home, Mumma made maple syrup and we had it over our pancakes in the morning. Other times, Daddy would take his jack-knife from his pocket and cut a piece of spruce gum from a spruce tree for us. I especially like to chew spruce gum, and once, when Daddy wasn't with us, I used my little penknife to cut a piece for myself. But when I started to chew, it stuck to my teeth. Little wonder—it was balsam! I soon learnt the difference between balsam and spruce, and to this day I never pass a tree bearing spruce gum without stopping to have a chew.

One spring, Garnet, my nephew, got into the business of trying to produce chickens by getting a little bantam hen. Bantam hens are as sassy as a blue-ass fly, but my nephew was not afraid of them. He got some bantam eggs from a farmer, turned an old barrel on its side, put a grass nest in it, placed the eggs in the nest and set the hen on the eggs until they hatched. Weeks later, on a beautifully hot day, we watched the eggs crack open and the chicks pop out. What a magnificent sight to behold!

Warm weather activities after school sometimes led children to mischief. And we were no different. One day my brother and four or five of his friends decided not to go straight home after school. They walked around the railroad tracks to MacKinlay Beach. Unknown to them until they took their shoes off and were wading in the river, I followed them. I took my shoes off and waded in with them. The tide was going out in the Avon River, which has one of the highest tidal bores in the world. We were having a barrel of fun sinking our feet into the mud flats. As a huge wave was going out, it started to take me out with it. Luckily, my brother was a good swimmer and he dove in and saved me. He immediately took me through Captain MacKinlay's yard and up the Shore Road to home. Not wanting to get my brother in trouble for my near drowning, we didn't tell Mumma the full story about this adventure until we were grown-up. Nevertheless, my brother was in trouble for taking me to the river and not coming home after school. This cost him a switching.

What a blessing when school was out for summer vacation! There was no catching a plane, train or bus to take a vacation in another city, province or country. Vacation time was spent swimming in the Half Way River and the Avon River. The community picnic was held at Arbadean Beach on July 1, Canada Day. The sidewalks in Hantsport were lined with people who had started gathering early to get a good place for the parade. There were marching bands, beautifully decorated floats, ox teams with harnesses, brass polished to a glittering shine and horse teams with ribbons in their tails.

When the parade ended, the picnic baskets were picked up and we were off to the beach for a day of fun, games and a huge picnic lunch. One year our family missed out on a part of the big day. Mumma had the picnic basket packed, but when we returned home after the parade, Daddy told us Mumma was sick and had to go to the hospital. Later that day we had a new baby sister. None of us wanted her. She had messed up our day! But, of course, when Mumma arrived home from the hospital with her, she became our little bundle of joy.

Many things happened in July. It was the time when we would wake up to the smell of clover in the fields and watch the farmers haying in their traditional way. They cut the hay with a scythe, raked it up with a hand rake and stacked it into piles to dry in the sun. Once dried, the farmers loaded the hay with hay forks onto the horse-drawn wagon. The hay was hauled to the barn to be stored for winter use. Farmers really believed in the saying "make hay while the sun shines," because wet hay couldn't be stored.

In warm weather, we played outside. One warm day, I must have been eight years old, three or four of us went off down Schurman's cow path to the Jud Spring. Mr. Schurman kept a big bull with a ring in his nose in a fenced pen. We were forbidden to go near his pen, but that didn't stop Mr. Schurman's grandson from going right up to the pen and screaming, "bull moose!" just as we were passing the pen. The bull started snorting and when we saw white froth coming out of its nose we turned and ran back home.

On stormy days we stayed inside with paper dolls cut out of the T. Eaton and Robert Simpson catalogues and the *Star Weekly*. We took time out from our cutting to look out the kitchen window at the big ships idling down the Avon River, going into the gypsum loading dock in Hantsport. Sometimes the sailors who came in at those docks got to know Daddy, a former shipyard employee who had an ongoing interest in the shipping industry. Often the sailors gave him a tour of their ship and he invited them home for dinner. When they came, like when all company came to dinner, Mumma and Daddy ate with the company at the first table setting and the children ate alone at the second setting.

Picking berries in season was a summer pastime. Trips into Riley's pasture among the thorny raspberry and blackberry bushes were not so pleasant, yet a lot of time was spent among these thorns, filling our containers. We always arrived home with containers and stomachs full of big juicy berries and fingers full of thorns. Once the thorns were removed and the day's adventures wound down, we saw from the dining room window Dickie's Hill reflecting the warmth of the setting sun, signifying the end of another day. During berry picking season the aroma of preserves filled the air. On just about every kitchen stove in the community was a cooking pot full of jam, jelly and preserves. We could be sure that Sunday dinner's desert was going to be Mumma's freshly baked home-made berry pie.

During my school years I was never aware of a double standard for black children and white, though sometimes my exams and even everyday school work appeared to be marked differently than those of my classmates. If my white classmates' answers weren't quite correct, they received marks for the portion that was right. On the other hand, if my answer was only partly correct, it seemed that the teacher gave me a much lesser mark. This method of marking was confusing to me and I asked my parents to explain it. They told me that sometimes I may have to know twice as much as some of my classmates. They never mentioned that I might have been marked differently because of my skin colour, so it wasn't exactly clear to me what my parents meant at the time. There was no way for me to know that they suffered the pain of racism and were trying to protect me from suffering the same at such an early age. Dealing with the effects of negative racial images, the fear of rejection, the fear of their children getting hurt and all sorts of outright racism must have been a challenge for Mumma and Daddy and the other black parents in Mount Denson. At an early age my parents provided me with positive exposure to non-black people, knowing that I would be dealing with them in order to achieve my goals in life. They raised me to believe that I am entitled to whatever rights are available to others. Perhaps they knew who the prejudiced community residents were and forbade us to play with their children. Regardless, I went to school and Sunday school and played with the white children in the community and never felt any fear of rejection.

The little two-room schoolhouse took the students up to grade nine. For their senior high-school education, students had to go to Hantsport High School. High-school text books were not free. Consequently, many poor families could not afford this expense and many children dropped out of school before completing their high-school studies. Some young people remained in the community to work on the family farm or do some work in the surrounding area; others left the little farming community of Mount Denson. At that time, a grade eleven education was considered enough for any ordinary person. Some went to the general hospital for nurses' training or to college. There weren't many professions open to women in those days.

My parents couldn't afford to cover the cost of a completed high-school education for their children. All the children in my family, like in many other families in the community, were forced to withdraw from school at age sixteen or seventeen, some to seek employment, others to help on the home farm or take on other responsibilities at home. My brothers were employed at the Minas Basin Pulp and Power Company. My sisters were domestic workers and helped out at home. When my two older sisters married, I was left as the oldest girl at home. I had to quit school in grade ten to babysit while Mumma went to work. In those days, high school was thought of as a luxury instead of a necessity. I wasn't surprised that I had to leave school because practically everyone my age was doing the same thing. However, my thoughts were that some day I would return to school because I wanted to get the highest level of education that I could.

There were certain traditions held in great respect by the community when I was growing up in the 1930s and into the early 1940s. Six days a week the farmers toiled the land, laboured and did all the work that had to be done. The women worked in the homes every day except Sunday, which was reserved for Sunday school and church. We attended Sunday school at Mount Denson Baptist Church. One of my favourite Sunday school teachers was Mrs. Alice Faulkner. She explained the Bible stories to us in a clear and understanding manner. She taught us the golden rule, "Do unto others as you would have them do unto you." We were taught in Sunday School that Jesus loves the little children and that we must love each other. When I saw a picture of Jesus, He looked so kind I truly believed He loved me and was watching over me. I wanted to love everyone and be their friend. I imagined everyone that died was living in Heaven with Jesus. Mrs. Peach was the church organist and there were two or three church deacons, one of whom delivered eggs to our house every Saturday. After his mother died he used to have Sunday dinner at our house. He enjoyed coming to our house so much that one Christmas he showed his appreciation to Mumma by giving her a set of fine china. Minister Scott made weekly community home visits, giving him the opportunity to visit each household at least once a year and giving us a sense that the church and the community were connected.

As a child, I was taught at home, at school, and at Sunday School that certain types of behaviour are expected from people who believe in God. We could not play games or dance on Sunday. We had to obey God's commandment to "remember the Sabbath and keep it holy." Sometimes on Sunday evenings some of Grammy Affie's white friends would gather in her parlour for a hymn sing. Aunt Edith played the organ and she always sang, "Sweet Hour of Prayer" and "Where Is My Wandering Boy Tonight." One of the most important things I remember about my religious upbringing is to love your enemy. There were a few times when a woman got mad at Mumma and wouldn't speak to her for a while. But then she would send one of her children to get a cup of sugar, a square of butter or some other item from Mumma and always Mumma sent it to her. When she called for a helping hand, Mumma went.

This was the forties. Nobody talked to children about issues like death, childbirth or sex. Whenever death came to our family or community, I would see Mumma wiping tears from her eyes, but I never saw anyone in a coffin nor did I ever attend a funeral. In our house no one dared ask questions and we were not allowed to be present when adults were talking. This was very frustrating for me as a curious child because there was no real conversation with my parents. They would just give a little talk—a sentence or two—on the issues they didn't want to talk about.

Whenever a funeral service was being held in the church, school was dismissed at noon. All children had to go straight home before the funeral service began at 2:00 p.m. If the undertaker came to place the deceased's remains in the church before all of us had reached home, we stopped until the undertaker's vehicle passed. When a member of a family died, it was the custom for family members to wear a narrow-black band around their arm. Women in the community used to bake sweets or make a dish and take it to the bereaved family's home. Grampy Charlie and Grammy Affie died just ten months apart. Grampy died March 6, 1942 and Grammy died January 8, 1943. When Grampy died, we children had to stay in the house until after the day of the funeral. Living next door to them we saw people in a car or two going in or out of their yard. These were sad times in our household. We could hear Grammy, Aunt Edith and some other people crying. Daddy only came into our house for a little while, then would leave again. He didn't even read the daily paper. I saw Mumma making black satin hearts and arm bands and putting them around people's coat sleeves. Daddy and Mumma wore these bands on their coat sleeves for months.

The Christmas after Grampy died, when Mumma dressed me up for our Christmas school concert, I went over to show Grammy how I looked. She pinned a beautiful little green pin on my green velvet dress and told me it was mine to keep forever. Mumma kept my pin in the little wooden box on her bureau. The day Mumma went to get it from the wooden box to give to me to keep, it was missing. I really missed Grammy when she died. Being a child, I didn't attend her funeral, but like Grampy's funeral, I remember Daddy dressing up in his navy blue suit with an arm band around his sleeve. I saw Grammy's coffin being carried out her front door and put into the long black hearse, and became so grief stricken I cried.

Grammy Becky died when I was seven. Grammy always carried her grocery basket on her arm when she took her daily walk into

invisible shadows

Hantsport. She continued her walks until three weeks before her death when she suffered a stroke. Grammy Becky was Hants county's oldest resident when she passed away on October 22, 1942 at the age of 104. The Town of Hantsport named a street after her, "Becky's Lane." I know it sure felt strange to pass Schurman's Road on our way to Hantsport and not stop into Grammy Becky's house. I missed her so much that when Mumma would take us down the cow path to Half Way River to swim, I would run ahead and stop at a certain little spot in a hollow on the side of the road that I referred to in my imaginary mind as Grammy Becky's house. Here I sat on a tree stump and waited for Mumma and them to catch up to me all the while pretending I was visiting Grammy Becky. Of course I didn't tell anyone why I stopped at this spot—they would have thought I was crazy.

The next close death in the family came when I was just reaching adolescence. Papa, my Mumma's father, passed away on January 7, 1948, and everything was odd at our house. Mumma wasn't home when we came home for lunch and she wasn't there to prepare supper. She went to Windsor Plains to be with her brothers and sisters. I only remember her being there one morning when we got up, but she didn't prepare our breakfast. I saw her wiping tears from her eyes, which made me feel very sad. My sister Ruby wouldn't let me ask Mumma why she was crying. I had to go off to school. On the day of Papa's funeral, Daddy told us he would be away from home that day. He told us Papa was dead and we must spend a quiet day at home. We were not allowed to attend school. No going outside to play in the snow or coast, and no playing the radio. We all felt so sad that Papa wouldn't be coming to our house any more to give us our big pennies.

Like death, sex was not something adults discussed in the presence of children; it was "adult talk." Nor was sex education taught in school. One day an older girl at school asked my friends and I if we knew anything about periods. We were very pleased and happy to tell her, "yes, they end a sentence." She informed us that there was another kind of period which she couldn't tell about, then gave us an address to send for a Kotex booklet which would explain it to us. Curiosity got the best of me and I asked Mumma if there was another kind of period. Her first reaction was "Who said this and what did they say?" Finding out that Joyce didn't tell my friends and I anything, Mumma told me, "Sometimes Joyce doesn't know what she is talking about and she is too old for you to be playing with." Needless to say, I didn't tell Mumma that Janice, Helen, Mildred, Glenda and I sent for the booklet. When it arrived, we gathered under the apple trees in Mr. Hunt's orchard. But, to our surprise, the material was like a puzzle written in another language. None of us had heard terms like menstruation, uterus or vagina. We looked these terms up in the dictionary and still couldn't understand their meaning. After wracking our brains trying to make sense of what we were reading, we finally realized the booklet was over our heads. Interest in this matter started to dwindle and was put on the back damper, until my oldest sister Ruth told me the other meaning of period.

I remember one summer in our adolescent years when we became interested in finding out about sex. Sex was something only married couples spoke about. As children, sex was in neither our vocabulary nor our interest. We were tossed out the door to play when Aunt Edith and Mumma wanted to talk about women's medical problems or any so called grown-up talk. Child-rearing and sex education were parental responsibilities. However, many mothers felt uncomfortable telling their daughters about the facts of life and so avoided the topic. A couple of years later, during a sister-to-sister talk with Ruth, she told me about sex, but she told me in a way that was not very clear to me at the time. I didn't tell her so, but I felt she didn't know what she was talking about.

In the 40s and 50s, when I was a teenager, pregnant women more or less stayed home. Pregnancy was a very shameful thing for unmarried women. There were homes for unwed white mothers but not for black mothers. Practically every black woman was already a mother or a mother-to-be on her wedding day. You rarely heard any talk about abortion. If it was practised, it was done illegally. There were no birth control pills or contraceptive measures practised openly then. If a woman became pregnant, she had the baby.

When I became a teenager I was under a very strict curfew and the urge to get away from the rules at home started to rise within me. The only socializing I did with my friends was going to a Saturday matinee at the York Theatre in Hantsport once in a while, and going skating or bicycle riding. I was not allowed to leave home after dark. If for some reason I did, one of my older sisters chaperoned me. I was not allowed to have lipstick, make-up or nylons. Most of my spare time was spent playing country and western records and dancing around the living room with my sisters and brothers. Really, I had very little time to socialize and no time at all to spend with boys. I thought of the things I wanted to do when I went out on my own: get a tube of lipstick, a pair of nylons and a boyfriend.

Spring was a time of romance and blood-stirring. When I reached age sixteen, I saw all the girls my age (and some younger) with real curls in their hair, lipstick, nylons and boyfriends. I began to question why I had to keep my hair in childish braids or use rag curlers to make ringlets. Then, I went to spend a weekend at my aunt and uncle's in Curry's Corner and they had a boarder who was a hair dresser. The day I arrived he was doing some black ladies' hair with Vaseline, a hot straightening comb and a hot curling iron. When he finished their hair looked so beautiful I wanted mine done too. Despite the hairdresser's pleading and my aunt's against the straightening, my final decision was to have it done. To say Mumma was angry is putting it mildly. To make matters worse, the heavy Vaseline in my hair made a breeding ground for lice. Needless to say, I never tried that again.

As I started to mature, I was allowed to stay up after my siblings went to bed. At these times I often enjoyed combing Mumma's hair and digging dandruff up on the bald part of Daddy's head and shampooing what little hair he had. On the other hand, Mumma kept adding more responsibilities to my list, such as ironing, sewing and embroidery work. Some of my parents' rules and regulations were difficult to deal with at the time. Nevertheless, I maintained a very good relationship with my parents at all times. Oftentimes later in life, when I went home for a visit and Daddy and I were alone, he told me I was a smart child and complimented me on being a hard worker. He told me not to worry about anything because there was going to be a Day of Resurrection for me.

I remember the first time my sister Mona and I were allowed to go to Windsor by ourselves. It stands out as clear in my mind as if it was today. She was nine and I was eleven years old. When we got off the bus in Windsor, the streets and stores were all lit-up with Christmas decorations and the sound of carols floated overhead. Walking the streets of Windsor, humming and singing Christmas carols, made us feel grown-up. We had two and a half hours to shop and only twenty-five cents each. We must have gone into just about every store to look around. What a blessing when we reached Steadman's Store and found the prices we were looking for. We went half and half on Mumma's gift—a cut-glass butter dish and cover that cost twenty-nine cents. Then we each got Daddy a handkerchief for ten cents apiece. One had blue polka-dots and the other one had red polka dots. Our Christmas shopping complete, we went home happy as larks.

My working ethic came from both of my parents. Starting at age fifteen, I took the initiative to make my own pocket money by selling all occasion cards, gift wrap, vegetable and flower seeds for the Gold Medal Company. It didn't take me very long to get rid of an order. I made a sale at just about every door I knocked on in the community. My parents were happy when I came back home with all my cards sold. I received a certificate with a gold metal star on it for selling such a large order. My parents were pleased and felt I was a great sales person. The money I earned paid my way into a Saturday afternoon matinee and allowed me to buy a treat or two for my younger brothers and sisters. It certainly wasn't enough to buy the kind of clothes I wanted, but it gave me a sense of responsibility and a sense that I was contributing to the family.

At the age of fourteen, a few years before making up my mind to leave home for good, I visited Cherry Brook, one of the Preston communities. Here, I had a frightening and perplexing encounter—my first real experience of colour consciousness. One Sunday night in June 1949, my older sister and brother-in-law came to Mount Denson to take me to their house in Cherry Brook. It was to be my first vacation away from home! The thought of going way down to Halifax County had my whole inside bubbling with excitement. This excitement started to change with the very car ride itself. The highway was so turny and narrow that a person could shake hands with a passenger in an oncoming car. It seemed like a never-ending ride to my sister's house. From Lake Banook, Dartmouth, there was nothing but woods on both sides of the highway. It was dark and scary. The first lights I saw were at Lovett's store on the Preston highway. Just a few yards down, on the opposite side of the store, we saw the lights from the Nova Scotia Home for Coloured Children. My brother-in-law told me we were almost home. The only lights between there and home were at the Hartlem's house, which set across the road from where the Graham Creighton Junior High School now stands.

Finally, we reached the house that would be home to me for the next two weeks. Upon entering and finding no upstairs, a lost feeling came over me. However, off the kitchen was a big, beautiful pantry with a table. This caught my eye as we only had a small under-the-stairs-type pantry back home. The real pleasure, however, was that I wouldn't have to share a bed with anyone. But, as I settled in for the night with no one in my bedroom to talk to, loneliness overtook me. Thankfully, tired from the long car ride and excitement, I soon fell asleep.

The next morning started with the sound of my brother-in-law's truck leaving for work. Before washing the sleep from my eyes, I went to the kitchen window and saw hens already walking around the backyard. It was a Monday, so I helped my sister wash the clothes after breakfast. While helping her hang them on the line, I gazed around as far as my eyes could see. Looking down the road from the lower end of my brother-in-law's fence, I saw Cherry Brook Bridge straddling Cherry Brook, which ran through the community. My eyes didn't fall on rows of apple trees like back home, though. Instead, wooded areas of huge pine, fir and spruce trees circled my surroundings. Across the road, several gigantic boulders added to an environment that looked much different from the cleared, flat open fields of Mount Denson.

After helping my sister, I sat down on the back step to rest. Other than the barking and yelping of dogs, all was quiet. This quietness gave me the opportunity to really observe my surroundings. People passing on the road, some with children, always smiled or spoke. I noticed the women wore bandannas or hats on their heads. The whole time I sat there, I never saw one white person pass by. I was used to seeing them back home and wondered why I didn't here. Throughout the day I didn't see any vehicles coming in or going out of the road. However, when we were preparing supper, I heard the sound of a vehicle, and went to the window to look. People were sitting on the back of a half-ton truck. My sister said they were coming home from work in town.

After supper my brother-in-law took us to Otto's ice house in Dartmouth to get a block of ice for the ice box. At that time, refrigerators were uncommon; the icebox was used to keep food cool. It had a place at the top to put a large block of ice and a drain pipe going down through it to drain the ice water into a pan under the bottom of the ice box. With the block of ice secured on the back of the truck, we started for home. On our way, we saw children at the Nova Scotia Home for Coloured Children playing on the swings. Passing the home, it struck me as odd that the sign read "coloured" children and not just children. When we got home, night fell, bringing a strong longing to be back home. My first glimpse of this community had left me feeling bewildered, and sleep took forever to come.

The following afternoon my sister took me for a long walk to Lake Loon. Along the way, the people we met walking or in their yard greeted my sister in a friendly manner. While passing some homes, we could see people peeking out of their windows. Just around the turn there was a house with an upstairs balcony on it and a well-maintained lawn. As we neared this house, a smiling lady came out to the road side to talk to my sister and ask who I was. She jokingly said, "You're in the sticks now child." She extended an invitation for my sister to bring me to meet her daughter, who was around my age. This put me at ease. Her friendly smile radiated a vision within me as to how friendly people in the community must be.

We continued our walk along the narrow, two-lane road leading in and out of the community. Huge trees with tangles of bushes under them bordered the road. Through these, we saw little ponds and water flowing in the gutters. Just around a turn, I saw a big brown animal standing under a wild apple tree in an open field. Of course, when my eyes got a glimpse of such a large animal with its big horns, I was scared out of my wits. When I screeched and grabbed onto my sister, the animal made one leap and disappeared out of sight. My sister said, "Don't be afraid. That was only a deer." When I asked her if we were going to see any more wild animals, she laughingly said, "No, these wooded areas make good watering spots for deer, but you usually just see them in the fall. They come out of the woods to eat the apples off the trees." At that moment, I decided to go back home to Mount Denson. To me this was a strange land that I couldn't place or define from geography learnt in school. I had certainly never had a school lesson on black communities in Nova Scotia. We turned at the Lake Loon Road to go back to my sister's house, but before reaching our driveway, we saw a big snake lying in the road, bathing in the sun. Startled by this long scaly creature, we hurried along home. Upon our arrival, I sat on the back steps thoroughly convinced that I had had enough vacation.

I was sitting on the steps watching the people going and coming, when for the first time I really took notice of the different shades of black people. Some looked like the few black people back home and some looked different. It was then that I became aware that Cherry Brook was a black community. Having seen a wild animal and not a single white person in this community reminded me of what I had learnt in school about Africa. A short section in our school text books about this beautiful continent left me with the idea that it consisted only of dark people and wild animals. I wrote a letter back home, telling my mother I was in Africa and asking her to please come and get me.

My day's experience brought a teary-eyed and sleepless night my way. I spent the next day reading and longing for home. After supper, my brother-in-law took us on another outing to get ice-cream at the Waverley Canteen. It was an exciting drive out the very narrow and winding Waverley Road, with rivers on both sides. Across the road from the canteen was a large cage with two black bears in it. I stood at a distance from the cage while my brother-in-law went right up to it. Just as he was drawing near the cage, one bear stood-up on its hind legs. Seeing this extremely large black bear standing up sent me back to the car in fright. However, I truly enjoyed the ice-cream and the twists and turns on the drive back home. This outing kept me content for the next couple of days. Still, I wanted to go home. I thought that being away from home would be great and would make me feel grown-up. However, I had not been prepared for the culture shock of life in a black community, nor for the good dose of homesickness that hit me. Upon returning to Mount Denson, I became aware of my lack of knowledge and understanding about my race. I realized that growing up in an over-protective family had made me immature concerning racial differences.

The happy-carefree times I spent with my white friends right through junior high school will never be forgotten. But when I became a teenager, my parents, especially Mumma, put a lot of pressure and restrictions on me. My mother gave me new responsibilities such as babysitting my baby brother, helping to prepare meals and perform other household duties. Most of my time was confined to working at home caring for my younger brothers and sisters, which meant I was not making any money to buy the clothes and things I wanted for myself. No going out at night to parties and movies, and dates were an absolute no-no. These restrictions allowed me very little time with my friends—it was almost as though I should only socialize within the family circle on Shore Road. These restrictions seem to have come from my parents' fear of the unknown, that is, the potential risk that too much socializing may lead to mixed couple dating. My parents, like many, considered marriage the ultimate goal in life for their children and put pressure on us to preserve our cultural identity. Many times I have heard my parents repeat, "People should marry their own kind."

Not fully understanding what this meant and not allowed to question my parents, I became annoyed with the way some things were at home. There was never a lot of emphasis placed on my broth-ers' roles in the household. They helped daddy carry firewood into the house and other than that they could do whatever they wanted. The day-to-day household chores and maintenance of the house were left to Mumma and the girls. Those were the days when men had a priv-ileged position in the home. This frustrated me and gave me a feeling of being cheated of personal freedom and individuality. I began to think it was time for me to take my own path in life.

Of course the only obtainable jobs I saw at the time in Mount Denson was apple picking in season. This wasn't my kind of a job, and I had no desire to hang around Mount Denson picking apples for a living. And so my lack of freedom and the need for employment were the deciding factors in my move to the Preston area of Cherry Brook. In 1953, I left home to spend the summer working at my brother-in-law's little store in Cherry Brook. While working there, I got to know some of the canteen crowd and went to some of the community ball games with them. One night a few girls and I were walking home from one of these games when we had a strange encounter with a police officer. It was twilight when a cop car stopped beside us. The cop asked us if we knew where a certain person lived in the community. None of the other girls answered. They dropped their heads and kept their eyes on the road, so I said, "No." He said, "You are lying. Everyone knows everybody around here." When I told him in a direct voice I wasn't from this community so maybe everybody knows everyone around here, he told me to get going because if he got me in the car I would know something. I became afraid and told the girls to come on before he took us to jail. After the car pulled away, the girls told me I was crazy to talk to a cop that way. As we continued on our way, the girls were moving almost at a running pace, trying to get off the road in case the policeman decided to come back. They told me: "You don't talk to white people." I couldn't understand why I had frightened them so by answering the cop's questions. This had been the proper thing to do back home where we respected the police for their protection of us. The girls' reactions and the abrupt tone of the cop's voice gave me an uneasy feeling.

After that encounter, I realized that we had all been black girls. By comparison, back home in Mount Denson, I was the only black one in our group. It began to dawn on me that colour had something to do with the way people were treated. This realization caused me to revise my outlook on life. Everyone I talked to about the incident felt that the police took every opportunity to arrest even the most law-abiding community citizens, just to demonstrate their power and authority. Coming from one of the smallest black populations in Canada into the largest indigenous black community in Canada, I had never encountered such prejudice and narrow-mindedness from white people. Community citizens, however, had a common knowledge and shared experience of racism and knew black people had little or no recourse under the law.

After living in Preston for a few years, when I got home at nights, I read the daily newspaper and followed the stories about the racial rumblings in the United States. Some of these stories began to hit home. They stirred a colour consciousness within me. The more I read, the more my curiosity grew. Little had I known that my genetic make-up was going to be a disability that determined who or what I could become. Because being colour-coded meant we were descendants of an enslaved people, we were kept economically confined and socially isolated.

An outpouring of writing on the American Civil Rights Movement continued in the daily newspapers. An article on the Montgomery bus boycott in 1955-56 especially drew my attention. The article stated how on December 1, 1955, Rosa Parks, a black woman, was arrested. She had refused to give up her seat to a white man on a segregated city bus in Montgomery, Alabama. Her quiet defiance inspired a bus boycott—thousands of black people joined together to demand equal rights for all. On December 21, 1956, the United States Supreme Court declared bus segregation unconstitutional, thus bringing an end to the boycott.

With little understanding of the social problems around race that existed in Canada, I was not prepared for the tragic challenges of the colour bar. The colour bar meant that black people were barred from everything except the barnyard. We were certainly barred from opportunities of employment. I had the surprise of my life the day I sought employment at Moirs' Candy Factory. When I went to apply, they asked me if I was black ("coloured" was the word everyone used then). When I answered "yes," they told me they didn't hire black people. Leaving there, I went to the Metropolitan Store and spoke to the manager (whom I later learnt was really the floor walker). He told me there weren't any jobs available, yet there was a "help wanted" sign posted in the window. The colour bar also applied when it came to public services. Black women couldn't have their hair cut or set in the white beauty salons, nor could black men get their hair cut in the barber shops. As a black woman, I found myself part of a society that didn't see me as a woman, but rather as a colour. Consequently, it was impossible for society to understand my value as a person. This created some disillusioning moments for me.

When I went to work at my brother-in-law's store, there weren't any other stores in the community at the time. His little store, known as "Bundy's Canteen," served the daily needs of the residents. It was a real pleasure for me to work at this canteen serving the friendly people in the community. It provided an opportunity for me to meet my neighbours and learn from the community elders.

During the day, business at the canteen was very slow, as the community men and some of the women were at work in Halifax and Dartmouth. On their way home from work, however, they stopped for milk, bread or whatever staple they needed at the time. In the evenings after the ball games, some young folks gathered at the canteen for a drink of pop, an ice-cream and a get-together talk. One of my most enjoyable times working there was during special Sunday services at the church. Whenever these special services were held, it was a sell-out of pop and ice-cream at Bundy's Canteen. Cherry Brook church held their most special church service—the baptism—on the fourth Sunday of July. The two neighbouring black communities of East and North Preston held theirs on the second and third Sunday respectively. It was at the East Preston Church Baptism in July 1953 that I met John Thomas, Jr. (Jackie). He was a ball player on Preston's ball team and he knew Elroy Sparks who played ball for the Cherry Brook ball team. Pointing to my brother-in-law's car where I was standing, John asked Elroy if he knew that girl over there. When Elroy told him, yes, John said he wanted to be introduced to me. We shook hands and he asked if this was my first time in Preston. Telling him yes, he said, "You're in God's country now." I thought he was a nice-looking guy but a little on the conceited side. Be that as it may, he told me years later that he told the boys he was with at church to look at his wife standing by the car. He said he knew the very moment he saw me that I was going to be his wife.

A few weeks later, we met at a ball game: Cherry Brook versus East Preston. He had a half-ton truck and drove the ball players to the games. Like in all sport games, some players had a loud mouth, but not John. I liked his style of playing. Following the game he came to the canteen and didn't talk much. However, from that evening on, he hung-out at the canteen a couple of evenings a week. It was as clear as crystal that he had a crush on me and it certainly didn't take long for him to ask me on our first date: to a Western movie at the Dundas Theatre in Dartmouth. After the movie, we went to the Harbour Café and talked a little over a banana split. I was impressed with his kind, gentle manner, yet a bit nervous that he may be a playboy. However, after a few dates, I realized that although he was only two years older than I, he was very responsible and mature. It was as if lightening

Moirs Candy Factory, Halifax. In the early 1950s, I was refused even the chance to apply for a job here because I was black.

invisible shadows

struck and a brilliant flash clicked inside of me saying, "this is the guy you left home in search of."

John became my strength during the difficult and trying times of adjusting to a new way of life. Wanting to make friends and fit into a segregated community certainly wasn't an easy task. When Bundy's Canteen closed for the winter, there was no way I was going to return to Mount Denson. Instead, I decided to stay and search for employment in Dartmouth. When I told my parents, they were certainly not thrilled. I wasn't surprised—my parents reacted the same way whenever any of their children left home. They wanted their children to become responsible adults, yet they never wanted to cut the apron strings. Nevertheless, my mind was made up. I had the feeling I was born for bigger and better things in life. I just didn't know what they were. I did know that I wanted to do something more challenging than housework and I had never wanted to marry my kinfolk. The time had come for me to leave my roots in Mount Denson behind and move on.

John (right) and his brother Lloyd, waiting for their mother to take them to church, ca. 1944.

After trying to find work at Moir's and other stores and being turned down because of my race, I turned to domestic work. A lady in the community doing domestic work got me a job with one of her former employers. This was a one-day-a-week job and do you know, that woman wanted two to three days of work done in one day. Washing a sink full of dirty dishes, making beds, dusting, vacuuming, cleaning, waxing and polishing hardwood floors, cleaning the bathroom, kitchen and down the basement steps was all to be done in one day. The hours were from 9:00 a.m. until 4:00 p.m., with a wage of $2.50 a day. If I didn't stop for lunch (a bowl of Campbell soup, placed at the side table), I finished at about 3:45. Although I went non-stop, the woman often asked me to do ironing until 4:00 p.m. I went to work two days a week for another woman who paid $2.25 a day, but she didn't work me as hard. Three days a week, during the cold winter, I drove in an unheated wooden cab on the back of a truck with other women from the community going into town to work.

In April 1954, on a chilly spring morning, I arrived to work for the first woman. She told me that she was entertaining that evening, so she had added a few more duties to my list. I was to polish the brass in the living room and clean out the fireplace. That did it! I thought very lowly of this white woman for asking me to clean ashes

John carried this photograph of me— taken at the Woolworth booth in Halifax, 1954—in his wallet before our marriage.

invisible shadows

from a fireplace. I had never cleaned ashes from our stove at home—that was considered men's work. So why did she think I would do it at this house? She told me her other cleaning woman did it and also did laundry. She wanted to know what was wrong with me that I couldn't do as she asked. Having recently read about how black folks were being treated like slaves in the United States and having learned about the long, hard working hours black women were putting into domestic work here at home, I stopped to think. This woman had been the beneficiary of slave labour and as such had placed a stigma on domestic workers. Suddenly, tension, caused by a feeling of humiliation, hit me. In a flash, I told her I would not be cleaning any ashes out of her fireplace, nor would I be cleaning for her period. I told her I was leaving. She told me I couldn't go, but I totally ignored her. Informing her that I would never become her slave, I took my coat and left her with a shocked look on her face and the thought of how she was going to get her house clean for the party.

This incident was like getting struck by a thunderbolt. I was engaged in a moral struggle: I had wanted to keep my employment, but I wanted to do so without losing my pride and dignity. In spite of black people's limited privileges and the difficulty of finding work, I refused to do any more cleaning or domestic work for any white woman as long as I lived. My mind was made-up: I would not participate in any society that was going to underrate my race of people. I had the hope that one day black people might share in the freedom and equality that other Canadians talked so much about. I didn't really talk to anyone about my new racial consciousness. This being the fifties, people in the Preston area didn't appear to have any knowledge or racial consciousness about the American Civil Rights Movement, and therefore it had no effect on their community at the time. Community leaders didn't take a stand on race issues and inequality because nobody was speaking out on these issues.

When John and I started dating, we had a typical teenage relationship. We went through a period of shyness and getting to know each other. He had a carefree, relaxed feeling about things, whereas I was sincere and nervous, still needing someone to lean on. He had a mature attitude that gave me the feeling he was really grown-up. Watching him and hearing him discuss things helped me become more independent. We had very few problems with each other. We just seemed to hit it off. We spent our time together at the movies, going to dances at the George Washington Carver Centre and just hanging out with the gang at Bundy's. One weekend when I went home, John came to Mount Denson to meet my parents. It was a Sunday afternoon. He was shy at first and didn't eat dinner with us, saying he had dinner before he came. Later, he told me dinner smelled so good and he hadn't eaten before leaving home, but he was too shy to eat with my parents. After sitting around talking for a while, he became more relaxed. Later, my parents told me they found him well mannered and thought he was a fine young man.

Mumma, like all mothers-in-law-to-be, had some reservations about what life away from home would be like for me. She only knew about Preston the negative things she had read in the newspapers, like the story of John's uncle accidentally shooting his wife in the leg during a dispute in their home, and the names of those going to court or jail for theft, fighting, bootlegging and other crimes. Regardless of any reservations she may have had, Mumma did a lot of baking for our wedding and within a couple of years her attitude towards Preston changed.

Personally, I had my own reservations about life in a black community. When I first moved to Preston, hearing stories about superstitious beliefs and the power of omens and witchcraft created some fear within me. But after living in the Preston area for three years, I got used to hearing these stories and was willing to settle into the community. This was a place where everybody greeted everyone they met and there seemed to be great community spirit among the people. Marriage was a mark of the times: an important symbol of accomplishment in the 1950s. Like all young ladies during that era, I fantasized about being married. After having kept company with Jackie for a year and a half, I began to envision raising our children so as to instil in them the same values my parents had instilled in me— belief in God, love and respect for all people. According to just about

invisible shadows

everyone we knew, John and I made the perfect couple; everybody seemed to feel that we would one day get married. John must have been very sure of this marriage also, because the night he proposed to me he had a beautiful diamond engagement ring ready for the occasion.

I felt happy as John and I began making plans for our future together: to have four children, to live in Preston, and to build a home. Yet, I still missed being at home with my parents. Each visit I made back home there was so much to talk about and our time together went so fast that I didn't want my visit to end. Since I wasn't living at home at the time of my marriage, my parents didn't get to know John very well. He visited my home in Mount Denson only a few times and most of that time was spent with my other siblings more than with my parents. This was an era when due respect for elders meant that young people avoided the company of older folks as much as possible, although John and Daddy would hold long conversations about farming at times. If John was visiting during Daddy's working hours, he drove Daddy to work or picked him up after work.

John and I knew both of my parents wouldn't be attending our wedding. That's just the way it was with my parents—both of them did not leave home for a long period of time. And overnight was a long period of time for my parents. John's parents had a similar sensibility. Daddy was giving my hand in marriage, so he got to come to the wedding.

November 9, 1956 was a beautiful fall day for a wedding. Everything was going fine until Daddy arrived at the house at about 2:00 p.m. After having a hot cup of tea and a smoke from his pipe, Daddy started to lecture me about marriage, telling me that I was entering into the state of holy matrimony, which bonds a man and woman together for life—something that should not be taken lightly. He wanted me to be sure that John was the man I wanted to spend the rest of my life with. He told me we would have our disagreements, which we would have to work out ourselves, but if John ever put a hand on me, I should tell him right away. Daddy made me so nervous I started getting scared. My brother-in-law Earl saved the day.

He took Daddy for a drive. While they were gone, I calmed down and my sister Regina, who was my bridesmaid, and I got dressed. Things were going great when Daddy and Earl arrived back. Shortly after, John's decorated car arrived and the driver, Wilfred Brooks, brought our flowers in—Regina's bridesmaid nosegay, Daddy boutonniere, and my beautiful bridal bouquet, all made from live flowers.

Our wedding was one of the first church weddings in Preston. The church was full when the car carrying my father and I arrived. The very minute my feet hit the church steps I became nervous and felt myself trembling. I shall never forget the church scene. Particularly vivid is my memory of the arch, decorated with wedding bells and evergreen, and of the bows on the church pews. While the organist played "Here Comes the Bride," my father led me down the aisle to the altar, where John was waiting. The closer I moved to the altar, the greater the trembling became, and petals from my bouquet fell to the floor with every step I took. The warm affection and love between us grew even stronger at that moment at the altar. After Reverend Skeir performed the ceremony, John and I went to Halifax for a drive before going to John's parents house where our reception was being held. The applause almost deafened me when John carried me across the threshold into his parents' house. There we performed all the rituals: kissing the bride, throwing the bouquet, cutting the wedding cake and opening gifts.

Weddings were special occasions in black communities. Whenever a wedding was taking place, community residents contributed to the feast. Someone would cook a ham, someone else would bake some sweets, another may give some pop and yet another might give some alcohol. These people were usually given a little special treatment at the wedding reception, such as being seated at a reserved table or being asked to give a toast in honour of the bride or groom.

Marriages took place at the bride's home or the pastor's residence in the evening. Many were married on Friday night and went to their customary jobs on Monday morning. There was no such thing as a honeymoon trip in those days.

Through Mumma's frequent visits to our home, she got to know the people in the community and very quickly forgot about the stories she read in the paper. During a couple of visits, I took her across the road to the school with me while helping my auxiliary sisters prepare for a fundraising dinner. Mumma had gone to school with two of these sisters, Mable Saunders and Marjorie Clayton. They put her to work helping them set the tables. She soon felt at home whenever she came to Preston.

I realized what a great life I was leaving behind in Mount Denson and the things I would miss: to wake up in the morning in my own bed to the sound of the farmers' tractors, to see the apple pickers picking apples from the trees, and just being able to communicate with my childhood friends. There would be no more swimming in the Avon River, no more going across the road to MacDonald's Candy Factory for peanut brittle, and no more visits to Aunt Edith's out the railroad track. I would really miss my time spent at Uncle Andrew's. These things may seem trivial to some people, but they were the things that brought happiness in my life and I would be leaving them behind. But with hopes of marrying and having a home and a family

Our wedding day, 1956. The wooden arch, covered with pine twigs, was made by Charles Colley. The arch and pews were decorated by Wilhelmina Riley, Georgina Harper, and others.

of my own caused me to think that the time had come for me to move on. The fact I had run into the problem of racism since moving to Preston didn't drain my hopes and dreams for the future. Oh, it made me feel disillusioned at times, but being the strong-willed person that I am, I knew I would overcome them. I looked forward to the life that I would be leading with John in the days to come.

When we were first married, John and I lived with John's parents and his eleven siblings in Preston. In the mornings, when John went to work, I had time to watch the children going to and from Partridge River School. In winter, the school children played on the little frozen pond between the schoolyard and John's parents' house. As I watched them playing in the yard, I quickly learnt that their play time often ended in childish feuds. Sometimes the mothers of the feuding children would get involved, then go about the community not speaking to each other. Before I knew it, the feuding kids would be playing together again, but their mothers remained "half-sideways" with each other. Sometimes this lasted for a few days or weeks, sometimes months, and even years.

From the sun porch I had a good view of the women going to and from their jobs as domestic workers in Halifax and Dartmouth. Some of them had a good mile to walk from Brooks Corner, where they got off the bus, to their homes on upper Brian Street. Brian Street was a secondary road, so during a heavy snowstorm walking was very difficult. John's mother was one of these working women living on Brian Street. If she was at work during such a storm, John's father would take the ox and drag to Brooks Corner to meet her getting off Zinck's bus. I often saw William Carter travelling past the house with his ox and drag, also on his way to meet the bus and pick up his wife.

Living in a house with so many other people afforded me the opportunity to get acquainted with my new surroundings. With so many sharing the household workload, there was time to sit around the huge floor register listening to stories about community life. William Dear, a well-to-do Negro man from the old days, was often mentioned. He owned a tourist house and barn at Brooks Corner known as the "Stag Inn"—the first inn run by a black person in Preston. It was sometimes used by Lieutenant-Governor Joseph Howe's carriage drivers. William Dear's sign read:

> The "Stag Hotel" is kept by William Dear,
> Outside, the House looks somewhat queer,
> Only Look-in, and there's no fear,
> But you'll find Inside, the best of Cheer:
> Brandy, Whiskey, Hop, Spruce, Ginger Beer:
> Clean Beds, and food for Horses here:
> Round about, both far and near,
> Are Streams for Trout, and Woods for Deer:
> To suit the Public taste, 'tis clear,
> Bill Dear will Labour, so will his dearest dear

William Dear died sometime during the 1870s, at which time his son George took over the running of the inn. When George died in 1895, the Stag Inn closed, although George's wife, Susan, lived there until her death in 1905. The building remained at Brooks Corner until the late 1940s.

The people who came to visit my in-laws told about how in earlier years Preston's mail was carried out to Joe Bost's by ox team. Joe had the Preston post office in his house. The post office was moved to Manette's, near the corner of Bell Street and Number Seven Highway, then to Sarah Clayton's. Later, it went to Florence Diggs, where it was at the time these stories were being told. The mail carriers dropped the incoming mail off on their way down the Eastern Shore and picked up the outgoing mail on their way back into Halifax. Due to heavy snowstorms the mail often arrived late during winter months, although delayed mail never created a big problem for Preston because letters from abroad were rare.

Some of the older women who came to visit talked about how hard they worked in Halifax and Dartmouth for their two dollars a day. They were constantly scrubbing floors, washing walls, cleaning windows inside and out (even in winter), and getting down on their knees to wax and polish the floors in the white woman's home. Sometimes they took old clothes and household articles in exchange for pay. After working hard all day they came home to do their own housework. They would hang their clothes on the outdoor lines by the light of a lamp held by one of their children. Many of these women had twelve, sixteen, or twenty children of their own.

One story I heard repeated several times was about the Halifax Explosion in 1917. The storytellers remembered this terrible disaster vividly. They said people in Preston didn't know what was happening. Homes and buildings shook as doors blew open and windows rattled, sending a fright over the community. Some residents gathered food and belongings and headed farther down the Eastern Shore to safety as they waited for the next blast, which of course never came.

The Stag Inn, Preston. In the last decades of the nineteenth century, travellers passing through Preston and mailmen going down the Eastern Shore spent the night at this inn, as did sportsmen taking advantage of nearby lakes, rivers and woods for fishing and hunting.

Today it is difficult to catch a glimpse of what Preston was like when I first arrived in the 1950s. Just about everybody in the community was of the same race and in the same financial situation, practised the same religion and had the same politics. It was clear that things in Preston were tough: big families and small incomes. Community residents had a house and a backyard, but beyond that, not much more than the bare necessities of life. Black folk lived on both sides of the Number Seven Highway, from Gough's corner to Bell Street, in homes that were on the whole small and run down. Unlike many newlywed couples of today, John and I didn't move into our own home on our wedding night. I must say I was a little apprehensive at first, living among so many people, yet I was optimistic that together John and I could face and surmount anything.

I had never been a morning person and wasn't used to waking up with so many people scurrying around the kitchen, talking about people and things I hadn't heard of. Even some of their language was different—"you them, cibbings and plat," I later learnt meant, "You fellows, bedding and braiding." Hearing the children laughing and joking in the morning as the older ones helped them get ready for school was strange to me. Back home, we children went to bed laughing and joking and woke up with a long face. Rarely did you hear laughing from us in the mornings. Before long, I got pleasure out of a bit of lively humour in the morning. During the evenings and especially on weekends, a lot of company, particularly men, came in. Through their visits I got to meet some community residents and they got to meet me.

When John and I started our life together, we began at rock bottom. John's bank account showed a few hundred dollars and mine held even less. I quit my job before I got married and my days were spent helping John's family with the housework. At the time, John was driving a truck and operating a power buggy for a construction company in Halifax during the day, and raising pigs with his father after work and on weekends. John worked from sunup to sundown saving money for a home. The little time he had for pleasure we spent skating on Partridge River and Dixon's Lake. We no longer attended social functions and dances at the George Washington Carver Centre or went to the movies. After our living expenses were taken out of John's salary, the rest was added to our savings account so we could purchase building material in the spring.

Before the first robin of spring arrived, John and I went to our bank in hopes of getting a loan to build our home. We had a good bank account (for those days), the car we owned was only three years old, and we were property owners with an excellent credit rating. However, the Bank of Nova Scotia refused us a chance to apply for a mortgage. This bank episode upset us to the point that we questioned why people in Preston were getting loans for cars but not for houses. Community residents' lack of collateral and a high rate of unemployment were among the reasons given. So this was why so many Preston residents were living in substandard housing, often without electricity and indoor plumbing. Their water supply came from nearby lakes and springs. A few wells provided drinking water for several families. Just about every home in the community was overcrowded. I first thought that community residents were lazy and could care less about their plight in life, but when I learnt the bank had red-lined the community, I realized it was different. We immediately and permanently removed our account from the Bank of Nova Scotia.

John took our money, built a garage, sectioned it off into three small rooms, and we moved in. This was a cosy little place, but it was sitting on cement blocks, not a foundation, so John put a sawdust banking around it to keep out the cold winter wind. A few homes had fir or spruce boughs around them. Our wood-coal stove in the kitchen kept the three small rooms nice and warm. John had plenty of wood in the backyard by the sawhorse and chopping block. John's father always got three or four loads of wood to John's one when they went into the woods together to cut wood. After the wood was sawed and split into stove-length pieces, we gathered up the wood chips to be used for starting fires in our kitchen stove. When John was at home, he kept a good fire in the stove, something I couldn't do. Every evening John sat with our oldest daughter, Wendy, in the big armchair given to us by Grandma Crawley. Before long they would both be asleep.

A typical day for me was taking care of my household chores, which didn't take a great deal of time since I only had three rooms to keep clean. My greatest task was taking care of my babies, sewing and knitting baby clothes, and doing laundry every day. I gave birth to seven children—three daughters and four sons. Unfortunately, once when I was about six months pregnant, I fell coming off John's parents' back doorstep. John rushed me to the hospital, but it was too late; we lost our son. John had Charles Colley make the baby's coffin and Reverend Skeir performed the burial while I was still in the hospital. John and I went through a difficult time that we talked about very little.

Over time, I came to know all the nooks and crannies of our little corner of the world and gained a sense of its history. John took me on frequent tours, always by a different route. We rode up through Glasgow Road, a connector road between East and North Preston, past Aunt Alice Ewing's house, onto Crane Hill. On the brow of this hill, just beyond a big tree, was the old Preston Cemetery, or what was left of it—a white farmer was growing vegetables on part of the cemetery land. People from East and North Preston once buried loved ones like John Wentworth Colley and James and Emma Neil in this cemetery, which had opened on June 26, 1791. Two huge vacant fields lay on each side of the cemetery; one belonged to Joe Saunders and the other was Thomas' Farm on Crane Hill. John's early ancestors, including James Thomas, the pastor ordained by Father Preston, once lived here. We drove along over this hill, eventually coming out onto New Road.

Our next tour was to Lake Eagle, first with a stop in the three vacant fields that once belonged to James, George, and Richard Carvery and that had been passed down to John's grandmother, Margaret (Carvery) Crawley. James Slawter, my next-door neighbour, told me that when he was a boy, he walked back to the little fishing town of Lake Eagle, where Preston's well-to-do Blacks lived. He said all the men out there used to fish, often catching enough both to keep and to sell. Families like the Carverys and the Downeys kept everything very neat and tidy. Richard Carvery had large crops of fruit and vegetables every year and when James visited, he'd be sent home loaded down with all kinds of produce.

The road into Lake Eagle was narrow and rough but still clear enough that we could drive right into Carvery's and Jimmy Downey's old fields. The scenery was beautiful. Wild apple trees and open fields lay around us. John took me to the edge of the lake and showed me where he used to fish. We shared tea from a thermos while I sat in a daze on the bank. Watching the big lake flowing crystal clear with the sunlight dazzling on it, I thought how very much Lake Eagle remind-ed me of the Bog Road back home. For years after, John and I took our children back to picnic and pick strawberries in July and August. My children all reacted differently to the woods we passed through before we got to the lake. Wendy, Wendell, and I were nervous, where-as Wanda and Miles, like their father, loved it. Cordell and Tina were too small to understand the difference. Once we filled our berry con-tainers, we went to the same shady spot where little tree tops inter-twined, making a canopy of leaves. Here we spread our blanket on the ground for our picnic lunch and listened to the birds chirping. After lunch, John and the children would roam about the fields, and I would sit on the bank of Lake Eagle and think of home.

The day we followed the little foot path leading from Grandma Crawley's house in lower Governor Street onto the old Crawley Road was a very short tour because the old roadway was covered with shrubs and bushes. When we first entered the woods on lower Governor Street, we could see George Glasgow's house, but it was soon out of sight. Walking along, sometimes stumbling over tree stumps and ruts in the road, I listened to the croaking of frogs in the nearby swamps. In a huge field, we came across the foundation stones of the old Crawley homestead. Many stone grave markers were close by. These neglected sites were remnants of the past, forgotten by the elders and virtually unknown to the young. The old road took us from lower Governor Street to Frog Lake Road. I made good time getting out of there, however, when we saw some large animal tracks. I learnt more about Crawley's Road from Albert Crawley and his sister Gertrude; they told me stories of how their family of three boys and five girls worked with their parents, Paul and Mary Crawley, on the farm. Because they kept a good number of pigs, cows, chickens and horses, Albert was up before the sun to help care for these animals. He told me many people in those days were buried on their own property and some of his family members, including his father, were buried in the field on Crawley Road.

Between pregnancies I continued to explore Preston. John's father told me about the old saw mills that once stood on lower Brian Street and the story about his uncle, Dick Ewing. One fall Saturday morning, Dick left home for Mill Pond to un-jam logs and float them downstream to the mill. When Dick failed to return home, his father, who came to Preston from the West Indies, went to the Mill Pond. When he didn't see any sign of Dick, the thought of his son falling off the logs into the water came to his mind. Removing all his clothes, he dove into the cold water in search of his son's body, which he didn't find. He caught himself a very bad cold, which he never got over, and some months later he died. In early May, Jimmy Neil went fishing in the Big Mill Pond and found Dick's body fastened by a log.

Old homestead ruins, Preston, 1959. Down lower Brian Street, I found bushes of beautiful red berries that I used for Christmas trimming.

invisible shadows

My first journey down Brian Street was in August 1959. Harris Brown came along with John and me on this tour of ruined and abandoned homesteads. All around there were signs of recent habitation. Huge fields surrounded every old foundation, and big apple trees were in just about every field. A variety of flowers and bushes was still growing in front of Richard and Alice Brooks' foundation, and a small broken fence still surrounded the flower garden. Alice Brooks told me stories of how she went with her mother by ox team to the city market to sell bouquets from this big flower garden. Piles of stones where fires were made in each foundation were still visible. The foundations themselves were made of stones, as were the long walls that separated each property.

Harris showed us where all the old folks once lived on lower Brian Street. Blue's and Dick Slawter's fields had grown very little. Behind a big tree by Sampson Carter's foundation was an old road used for hauling lumber. Carter's Pond was also on this property, and Huckleberry Hill was in behind Annie Johnson's field. Harris showed us the homestead where he had been born to Joe and Cecilia Brown.

Oxmobile, ca. 1920. Preston vendors carried goods by ox and wagon to sell at the city market or peddle about the streets.

(Cecilia was one of Preston's midwives.) We walked for miles on end, passing several lakes and ponds with large hills and mountains in the background. We saw the ruins of Gilbert Murry's Mill, Ginger Smith's Mill, and the big mill way back by the Big Mill Pond, later known as Wisdom Mill Lake. During one of Alice Brooks' visits to my home, she recalled getting lost on Wisdom Road. She went berry picking as a young girl from her home on lower Brian Street, walking way, way down, stopping to pick berries here and there. Without knowing it, she had turned onto a road she'd never been on before and walked so far along she lost all her familiar places. Looking around, she suddenly realized she was lost. Instead of turning back, she kept travelling and just before dusk fell, she came out of the woods in Porter's Lake. From there she knew her way home and certainly made haste in getting there. She arrived home, tired from her experience. She never forgot where Wisdom Road was!

Reaching Trimble's Lake with John and Harris, we rested and ate lunch before looking around the site. There, about three miles back from lower Brian Street, in a very large field, we found William Trimble's headstone and some other grave markers. At a distance, we could read the epitaph:

Trimble's field, 1959.

At Rest
In Memory
of
William Trimble
Died
May 4, 1887
Aged 57 years
Forever With the Lord

We stood on Trimble's bank and looked for miles up the large, beautiful lake before heading back home. These frequent ventures were tremendously rewarding for me. Wildflowers and weeds inhabited the deserted fields, and the ruins of old homesteads, gravestones, and rusted tin cans brown with age were visible reminders of the old days. It was amazing to still be able to see where Crawley's Road, lower Brian Street going past Trimble's field into Wisdom Road, and the old Preston Road leading into Bell Street were tramped into the rocky soil of Preston by its early settlers. These were now no more than old roads and swamps blurred by new growth, many just the ghost of a footpath. But they took me back to Preston's roots.

After an outing it was always good to come home to our humble little hut and sit in the big armchair until it was time to prepare supper. After supper, John and I would sit in our little sitting room and discuss our day's exploration of this tree-covered wilderness, where there was a blessedness of fresh air and no corner where the sun couldn't reach. I remember looking into the lakes and rivers full of trout, eel and gaspereaux, smelt and perch, and thinking how the real richness of a community lies in its people and its past. Some days I just sat under a tree and wondered about how the first settlers felt when they arrived in Preston, this place so different from my Mount Denson home. I continued to seek out community elders, who told me stories about the religious beliefs and customs that belonged to their African ancestors and about how slaves used secret codes and symbols to enable their escape. Even Negro spirituals were used to hide information that could be of help. "Follow the Drinking Gourd," they told me, was a coded map to Canada, and symbols encoded in patchwork quilts, with their square knot, monkey wrench, wagon wheel, bear's paw, star, and other designs, provided links to the Underground Railroad. At the time, I had no understanding of the cruelty and horror of slavery, but I sensed pain in the voices of those telling the tales about how they got here.

The first known black person to come to Canada was Mattieu da Costa, a former Portuguese slave who arrived in 1605 with the expedition of Pierre de Gua, Sieur de Monts, founder of Port Royal. The French settlers at Port Royal, who were trading in animal furs and skins with the Mi'kmaq, named da Costa their interpreter with the

Mi'kmaq. Some African slaves from the thirteen colonies of Britain were imported to New France to be used by wealthy white plantation owners and their families. The men usually worked as field hands, the women in domestic labours.

In the late seventeenth century, black slaves began arriving in New France in significant numbers and, by 1689, the French had established slavery in Quebec. Louis XIV issued a royal mandate which gave colonial settlers permission to avail themselves of the services of African slaves. This form of bondage made it possible for black people to be listed as slave owners' property. This system remained unchanged when the British conquered New France, as evidenced by the articles of the Capitulation of Montreal in 1760, which guaranteed French and British residents the continued ownership of their slaves. Both the Peace Treaty of 1763 and the Quebec Act of 1774 reconfirmed the articles regarding the ownership of slaves. In 1759, more than one thousand black slaves arrived in New France; some were sent on to Louisbourg on Cape Breton Island. In 1767, the first census showed that black slaves had lived in Halifax since the city's founding in 1749. Of Nova Scotia's 3,000 residents in 1767, 104 were listed as slaves. Advertisements in local newspapers like The Weekly Chronicle and the Nova Scotia Gazette offered rewards for the capture of runaway slaves, bequeathed them in wills, and sold them like livestock. On May 30, 1752, the Halifax Gazette ran an advertisement for the sale of "a very likely wench, two boys and three men." On March 28, 1775, the same newspaper had an advertisement for the sale of "a well-made Negro boy, about sixteen years old."

During the American Revolutionary War (1776-1783), the British began to bring both black and white Loyalists into Nova Scotia. As a means of weakening the thirteen colonies' economy, during the American Revolution Lord Dunsmore (the British governor of Virginia) promised freedom to any slave who joined and fought on the British side. Several thousand Blacks formed British brigades such as the Black Pioneers and the Ethiopian Regiment and fought hard to earn their liberty. When the British lost and had to be evacuated between the months of April and November of 1783, 2,775 Blacks

invisible shadows

were selected for removal to Nova Scotia, gaining freedom at last through the provisional peace agreement between Britain and its former colonies.

Immigration increased from 1782 onwards, and at the peak of this exodus from the American colonies, black Nova Scotians constituted at least ten percent of the province's population. The British government promised the same to the black Loyalists as it did to the white: land, provisions, and fair treatment. In 1783, the British shipped about 4,500 black Loyalists to mainland Nova Scotia. Approximately 3,500 were free, while, paradoxically, 1,000 were enslaved to white Loyalists. Many of these slaves, often referred to by the British as "servants," had fought alongside their masters.

Three hundred Loyalists joined black settlers to weave the fabric of a settlement in the rural setting of eastern Dartmouth. In 1774, this settlement was named "Preston" by British Army Officer Captain Robert Preston, who had been stationed in Boston during the American Revolution and who owned land near Governor John Wentworth's farm on Governor Street. In 1784, Governor Parr of Nova Scotia ordered Theophilus Chamberlain, under the direction of Surveyor General Charles Morris, to survey Preston as a township. Preston's boundaries extended from Old Dartmouth (Graham Corner) to Chezzetcook—land that the Mi'kmaq had lived on, hunted and fished for centuries. The newly surveyed township included what we know today as East Preston, North Preston, Cherry Brook, Lake Loon, Montague Mines, Preston (later known as Westphal), Porter's Lake, Lake Echo, and Ross Road.

Theophilus Chamberlain and 163 others were granted lots on October 15, 1784. To the Loyalists, the British government had promised one hundred acres of land per civilian family head and fifty acres for each family member; however, of Preston's three hundred black Loyalists, only fifty-one received land grants—2,557.5 acres total for the fifty-one individuals. And the land was the rockiest and most unfertile in the woods at Preston.

While their white neighbours were given lands grants outright, the black Loyalists were given only a licence to use their plot of land

and therefore could not sell it to purchase better land elsewhere. The licences came with a six-year waiting period and were conditional on land improvements. The majority of those who received land grants made the improvements, clearing the land and building huts to shelter their families from the cold Nova Scotia climate. Those who failed to make the required improvements had to forfeit their land. Black settlers could also not afford survey costs, so many of them didn't know where their property began or ended.

Included in the survey of land intended for the black Loyalists were two hundred lots Chamberlain had surveyed and marked out for a road. The black settlers immediately began to clear trees and rocks to build this road—they knew it was badly needed for transportation to and from Dartmouth. While the road was being built, they carried their weekly provisions eight or ten miles on their backs home from Dartmouth. This road would also prove useful in transporting agricultural products to the Halifax market.

While the black Loyalists in Preston were doing their best to create a good environment for their community with roads, shelter, and a school, it wasn't long before they were joined by more Blacks. On April 9, 1785, 194 free blacks arrived in Halifax from Saint Augustine, many of whom settled in Preston. Upon their arrival, the governor asked for clothing and rations from the military stores for the relief of these destitute newcomers, but the authorities provided only meagre

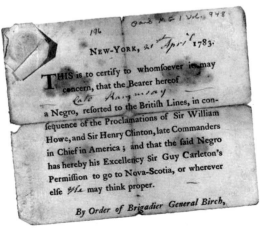

This certificate of freedom was issued to Cato Ramsay by General Samuel Birch, after whom the black settlement of Birchtown was named.

food rations, a few warm pieces of clothing, and a few tools. Perhaps they thought these people would die from the approaching winter and cease to be a problem. Instead, newcomers cleared away trees and rocks, built their huts, and—with the help of those already living in Preston—survived. What a surprise the authorities got in the spring when they saw this crude but thriving community!

While some Blacks settled in Preston, many others settled in Birchtown on the outskirts of Shelburne. The British Brigadier General Samuel Birch issued a freedom certificate to any Black who had been a refugee for the past year. One group selected to emigrate to Nova Scotia was the unit of troops known as the Black Pioneers. This "Brigade of Blacks," totalling 1,500, arrived at Shelburne in August 1783 and helped to lay out and build the new town. They also set up a town site for themselves on the north-west fringes of Shelburne, which they named "Birchtown" in gratitude to General Birch. Birchtown became the largest settlement of free Blacks in the world, outside of Africa. During this period, roughly thirty thousand people were looking for help and it was almost impossible for the government to supply them with the essential goods and materials they needed to live. There was suffering by both the black and white Loyalists, but the suffering of the Blacks was great enough to force a number of them back into slavery to survive.

Loyalist preacher David George was a pastor in Shelburne and did much to comfort the residents of Birchtown in their suffering. Born a slave in Virginia in 1742, George made two attempts to escape from his severe master; with the help of a tribe of Natchez Indians, he was successful in his second attempt. Four years after his escape, some white children loaned him their school book and taught him to read. George was a Baptist preacher living in Charleston, South Carolina when the English evacuated it at the close of the revolutionary war. The English gave him his papers and free passage to Nova Scotia. At Shelburne, in June 1782, he began preaching the gospel to Blacks in Nova Scotia.

Out of necessity and a desire to gain real freedom, black Loyalists began to protest to the government in Nova Scotia. After years of waiting, they were convinced that white officials had no intention of fulfilling the promise of equal treatment with their white counterparts. They became disillusioned with what they hoped would be a land of freedom and eventual independence. When they found there was little response to their protests in Nova Scotia, one of their black leaders, Thomas Peters, went to London to present their grievances. There Peters met a group of Englishmen who had recently founded an anti-slavery society that promoted a colony in Sierra Leone, West Africa. Peters returned to Nova Scotia carrying a promise of free land and all the rights of a British citizen for black Loyalists who chose to go to Sierra Leone. Faced with the setbacks of oppression, neglect, agricultural failure, and a slave society, many black settlers answered the call to immigrate to Africa. On January 15, 1792, Thomas Peters, David George, and about 1,100 black Loyalists sailed from Halifax to Sierra Leone to start a new life.

Another group of early black settlers was the Maroons, who came to Nova Scotia from Jamaica. The island of Jamaica was invaded by the Spaniards in 1494, and remained in their possession for more than a century and a half. In 1655, when the British conquered the island, most of the Spanish inhabitants moved to Cuba. However, many of their black slaves—descendants of African slaves—escaped and fled to the mountains. Known popularly as the Maroons, they were a brave race of people who lived for generations in mountain fortresses that were almost inaccessible to the whites.

In 1795, war broke out again between the Maroons and the colonial government. After six months of fighting, the government decided to uproot the group and drive them out of their mountain fortresses. The Maroons eventually surrendered as prisoners of war on the condition that they not be removed from Jamaica. On January 1, 1796, this condition was breached by the Legislature of Jamaica, which voted to exile the prisoners. One group was to be deported to Nova Scotia and two commissioners, Alexander Ochterloney and William Quarrel, were sent from Jamaica to supervise. Instructions from England were given to Sir John Wentworth to make provision for their settlement in Nova Scotia and the Jamaican government acquired five thousand acres of land in Preston to this end. The Jamaican government spent three thousand pounds of Jamaican currency on land and buildings and another twenty-five thousand pounds were given by the island government to the credit of the new settlement. Later, the British Government gave an allowance of 240 pounds a year to support a school and religious training for the Maroons.

On June 6, 1796, three large ships carried 556 exiled Maroons out of Port Royal Harbour, Jamaica bound for Nova Scotia. Fifteen days later, three ships—the *Anne*, the *Dover* and the *Mary*—made their way into Halifax Harbour. Temporary shelter for the group was provided wherever it could be found. Fifty of the new settlers were placed in old barracks on Governor Wentworth's farms, while others spent their first couple of months in Halifax, building and renovating Citadel Hill.

Soon after the Maroons arrived several estates in Preston were purchased for their settlement, one of which was the Preston summer cottage of Halifax sheriff Francis Green on Montague Road. The cottage was reconstructed and enlarged to a ten-room, two-storey house for three thousand pounds sterling at the expense of the Jamaican government. This building became "Maroon Hall." Along with another tract of land leading from Sir John Wentworth's property (Governor Street, East Preston) into the settlement of New Road (North Preston), this estate became home to the Maroons.

Once the Maroons were settled, they organized into military units similar to the style of self-government they used in Jamaica. Governor Wentworth of Nova Scotia appointed captains and majors among them and ordered officers' uniforms for their use. Among the recorded names of Maroon officers are colonels Montague and Johnson.

Unfortunately, these great fighters and workers lived only a short time in Nova Scotia. Failing to grow bananas and yams on their farms in Preston, they were disheartened both by the withholding of their supplies and the severely cold winters which affected their diet and habits. The winter of 1798-99 was even colder than the preceding ones and their number diminished as their graveyard filled. Faced with isolation, infertile land, racial intolerance, and the militant opposition of white labourers, the black settlers found it difficult to become self-sufficient. Money granted by the Jamaican government for their support was running out. They protested to the Imperial government to fulfil its promises, then petitioned the British Parliament requesting to be removed from the situation. Negotiations between the Imperial authorities and the Sierra Leone Company took place, and the company agreed to take the Maroons to help them quell a local uprising. On August 3, 1800, the *Asia* sailed out of Halifax Harbour, carrying many of the Nova Scotia Maroons to Freetown, Sierra Leone.

The third large influx of black people came to Nova Scotia during and after the War of 1812. The British again offered freedom to runaway slaves who joined them, and between 1813 and 1816, nearly two thousand black refugees came to Nova Scotia. Some of them eventually settled in Preston on the lands left vacant by the 1792 Loyalists' migration to Sierra Leone. Unlike the earlier black Loyalists, these former slaves lacked leadership and education, which made it difficult for them to face the existing economic distress and Nova Scotia's cold climate.

Several hundred of the new arrivals were black refugees from Chesapeake, one of the first regions in the United States to which Africans were sold as indentured servants and slaves. In 1813, the British Navy moved into Chesapeake, and on September 18 of the same year the *Acadia Recorder* announced the arrival of several British warships in Halifax. On October 2, 1813, one hundred and thirty-three Chesapeake Blacks arrived. These refugees came, fleeing the calamities of war to seek asylum under the protection of the British government. Like their forerunners, the Chesapeake Blacks were promised land grants and freedom. Unfortunately, they too were thrown into a relationship of economic dependence with white society. These black refugees were severely unemployed and poorly housed, fed, and clothed. The result was a vicious circle of limited opportunity, poverty, and low status.

In 1815, the care of the black refugees was placed in the hands of Thomas Jeffrey, the Collector of Customs, who had access to the Melville Island Depot. Originally used as a compound for American prisoners-of-war (who were released when peace was announced in

1815), Melville Island Depot was converted into a hospital. Between April 27 and July 26, 1815, Jeffrey placed a total of 727 newly arrived black refugees there. Hundreds of other black refugees from the Halifax Poor House and those arriving on ships from the United States were also admitted to the Melville Island establishment where clothing and rations were issued to them.

As additional numbers of refugees arrived in Halifax, many continued to be placed on land procured for their settlement in Preston. On September 6, 1815, Surveyor General Charles Morris reported to the Lieutenant Governor that there was a tract of land available in Preston where they could place two hundred Chesapeake refugee families. They issued food, clothing, and tool rations, and gave the refugees licenses for eight- to ten-acre farms. The government's hope was that the settlers would supply the nearby Halifax market with vegetables. However, crop failures prevented the settlers from becoming self-supporting. They were housed in bark tents and received rations for only a few months rather than the three years they had been promised. Chamberlain and Morris, agents for the Blacks, were ordered to withhold the allowance of those who were not building a house. (See Appendix A.)

These early residents found themselves in what was one of Canada's least developed and most economically fragile settlements. The negative effects of the culture of poverty set limitations on the community's development and growth. Not until after Theophilus Chamberlain's report of May 9, 1816 were they given full rights to their property.

The black settlers at Preston continued to clear land, build accommodations, and make other improvements. On May 10, 1816, the Lieutenant Governor arranged to have all the healthy black people removed from the Melville Island establishment to join other settlers in Preston. At the end of 1816, there were 924 Negroes settled at Preston—319 men, 258 women, and 347 children. The refugees shared many similarities and basic motivations with their predecessors, the black Loyalists, and soon the two groups merged to form the community of Preston, the largest pioneering black settlement in

Nova Scotia. However, until 1842, Blacks in Preston were still without deeds to their property. It was the granting of these deeds in 1842 that finally gave Preston residents a sense of kinship in Nova Scotia.

In 1820, twenty years before deeds to property were given, the British government and the Governor of Trinidad agreed that refugees who wanted to leave Nova Scotia would be shipped to Trinidad and given land. This suited both governments, as there was a shortage of labour in Trinidad, and the British Government was only too happy to stop supporting the black refugees in their care. Interestingly, despite reneged promises, cold climate, poor land, prejudiced attitudes, and other hardships, the majority of black settlers stayed—though this may have been out of a fear of being thrown back into slavery, which existed in the British colonies until 1834. In 1821, then, less than one hundred refugees went to Trinidad. Of those who stayed, their faith, hard work, and desire to succeed allowed them to pass down land and the hope of a better future for those to follow.

Almost two hundred years later when I came to live in Preston, black people were still living in separation from whites. Reading about the segregated laws and bus boycotts in America during this time, I looked for the signs of separation between blacks and whites in our capital city of Halifax. Being a curious person, my first thought was to take a ride around Halifax on the trolley coach. No sign was posted to say black people had to sit in the back of the bus, but nine out of ten black people did go to the back. The passengers' and the drivers' attitudes made it evident that black people weren't fully welcome aboard, and white passengers only took seats next to black passengers if no other seat was available.

My trolley ride through the south end of Halifax brought me face to face with the city of my dreams: huge trees with evenly kept branches, paths of flowers here and there along the sidewalks, mansions with well-kept lawns and flowering shrubs, and hospitals surrounded by trees and well-maintained grounds. The beautiful Public Gardens truly caught my eye: colourful flowers everywhere, birds picking around the ground, and swans in a small pond. However, as the trolley made its way around the many streets, I discovered some amazing things that history had neglected to reveal about the capital city—the manner in which the black presence was established within it in particular. Blacks were concentrated in the north end and the downtown area along Barrington, Creighton, Maynard, Gottingen, Gerrish, and Cornwallis streets. On the hillside slopes facing the Bedford Basin, I saw Africville from a distance: a model of the dominant white strategy for separating and confining Blacks in the capital city.

I got off the trolley coach and went on a walking tour. Just over the hill from the abattoir, next to the city dump and forgotten by the city politicians, I came upon Africville. Walking along the railroad track and unpaved streets past open wells and outhouses made me wonder: was this the city I had longed to explore? Later, when I returned with John to meet and visit Uncle Leon and Aunt Emma, I was to learn that only after Africville had been settled did the city run railroad tracks through the community, set up the city dump there, and refuse to pave the streets or extend water and sewage services. And the people in Africville paid their taxes just like people in the South End. After just one visit to Africville, it was clear to me that the city wanted to make life miserable for these people.

A beautiful scene greeted me at the Public Gardens on my tour of Halifax's South End in the 1950s.

Seeing lines of washed clothes blowing on outside clotheslines and small flower and vegetable gardens growing in people's yards gave me the sense that the community was concerned about its surroundings and determined to press forward in spite of the city's mistreatment. The well-maintained homes, hospitals, universities and other institutions that I had seen in Halifax's south end faded from mind as the deplorable conditions of the north end and of Africville took over. My fear of rodents was stirred when I caught a glimpse of the rat races going on in and out of the alleys around the Africville dump. The visit ended with a strong feeling of revulsion, but with it came a clearer sense of consciousness of my race. It was obvious that the city was separated into neighbourhoods, white and black. Catching the ferry from Halifax to Dartmouth, I found black folks congregated in one section of the ferry. The separation of black and white people seemed to be everywhere. Returning home that evening to Preston, I told John about my day's experience. He assured me that I would find the same

Africville, ca. 1962-1966. Although there were some well-maintained homes in Africville, most of the community stood in stark contrast to the picture perfect south end of Halifax.

invisible shadows

type of separation in Preston: black people in the middle bordered by groups of white people on both sides.

Hearing the folks of Preston refer to themselves as descendants of slaves, the words "slavery" and "slave" lingered in my mind day and night, but never more so than when the City of Halifax started targeting Africville for demolition in the mid-1960s. Listening to the people of Africville speak out, I learnt that they too were descendants of free African slaves. John and I couldn't believe Aunt Emma and Uncle Leon's beautiful home was to be torn down. The terrible destruction of their community sent shivers up my spine. We watched homes being bulldozed and residents' belongings being hauled away in city dump trucks. People took a stand to remain in Africville and defend the community they had built, but when they awakened one morning to find their church had been bulldozed during the night, they realized the end had come. Much against their will, the community's eighty families were moved, many to public housing in Halifax. Just as slaves were taken against their will from the shores of Africa and brought to the New World, so too were their descendants, the residents of Africville, uprooted against their will and re-located.

The longer I lived in Preston, the more I began to realize that the poor living conditions there had to do with something outside the community's control. Two eating establishments in Halifax and Dartmouth were frequented by black people—the Mayflower Café on Gottingen Street and the Harbour Café on Portland Street. When my youngest sister came to visit from Mount Denson, I took her to the larger and fancier Shell Restaurant further down Portland Street. The moment we entered, all eyes fell on us. We sat for fifteen minutes watching the waitresses serve other people (some who had come in after us), stand idle, talk to each other, and stare at us. Finally, I asked for service at our table, and heard one waitress ask the other, "Are they coloured?" The one that answered, "I don't know," came to serve us. She tossed the menu and silverware on the table with such an attitude that my sister and I told her in a very pleasant manner, "We don't associate with ignorance and rudeness, so there is no reason for us to stay here and pay for it." We got up and walked out.

My next encounter with this kind of problem was at the Community Grocery Store on Portland Street. While in line at the meat counter, there were some black folks as well as several white folks ahead of me. I watched as the meat cutter picked beautiful, fresh-cut meat out of the display case for the white folks, whom he treated with respect. To the black women, he made fresh jokes ("I know you want rump meat," he said), and went to the meat-cutting table, picked out a piece of darker, tainted looking meat and placed it on the scales for them. He was certainly not pleased with me when I pointed out the specific cuts of meat I wanted to purchase. He over-looked the pieces that I pointed out and picked out tainted cuts. When I told him that I was capable of picking out my choice of meat, he still reached for pieces at the back, underneath or to the side before land-ing on the piece I wanted. Disgruntled, he weighed, wrapped, and priced the meat, passing it to me with a look of contempt.

This type of treatment followed me into the holiday season. At Christmastime when my friend and I went shopping, the sales clerks at Robert Hall and Price Masters in Dartmouth made it obvious they were watching the black shoppers. The same happened at the Metropolitan Store on Barrington Street in Halifax, with the sales clerks peeking and peering at us. While they were busy watching the black shoppers, I saw a well-dressed white woman in a beautiful fur coat pick up a pair of pink women's slippers, put them in her hand-bag, and walk out. This incident was like a Christmas bonus to me. I thought, good for you—while you're watching others, your own is walking away with the store.

Upon arriving in the Preston area, it didn't take me long to realize that I didn't have any comprehensive knowledge of the completely different set of circumstances I was living in. I began to seek ways and means to shed light on the questions that my head and heart were ask-ing. How long have these communities been in existence and why are people still settled here? There were major kin groups in Preston, yet few real friendships seemed to exist. Gossip, verbal abuse and arguing among the residents caused tensions. A friendly rivalry seemed to sep-arate the three Black communities—Cherry Brook/Lake Loon, North

Preston, and East Preston. Each community had its own sense of identity. Cherry Brook/Lake Loon had a desire to mirror society at large and a sense that prosperity could be gained from social contact with white people. North Preston was a tightly-knit community sustained by its own culture, lanaguage and identity and with little desire to move beyond its own boundaries. East Preston saw the importance of blending with other communities. But an even greater social distance separated the black communities from the white ones. People who married into one of the "other" communities were looked upon as outsiders. There were days my stomach was tied in knots wondering if I would ever understand this community.

As I suffered through the pain of adjustment, I looked to the black community for strength and encouragement. Much to my surprise and bewilderment, I was confronted with another kind of oppression, this time from my own race. I began to realize that the issue of race among many black people was in fact skin deep: if you were light-skinned, as I was, it meant you had a white bloodline you couldn't deny, no matter how black you felt on the inside. Black people have a lot of racial names for people like me: mixed, high yellow, squaw, zebra, mulatto, pale face, half-breed and, more recently, bi-racial. I was not the stereotypical black woman that whites in the surrounding area wished to have around. I was a half-breed outsider.

It was difficult trying to take root in a community where people judged me, as Martin Luther King Jr. said, by the colour of my skin before knowing the content of my character. And I couldn't understand why many of my race hated me for being a little different and wanting more out of life than what the white world offered us. I knew I was black and never made any effort to hide or deny it. Therefore, I felt betrayed not only by white society for the blatant racism I faced when seeking employment, but also by the difficulties I suffered from being judged the wrong shade of black by other black people. I learnt that betrayal cuts deep no matter what colour the betrayer is. At the same time, I recognized that racism in the white society prevented me from educational and employment opportunities, whereas the oppression caused by black society didn't. As all black people, they were as powerless as I was. There were barriers in Preston penning black folks in. These barriers couldn't be crossed without intimidating white people, so Preston's blacks got used to living within them—rarely questioning store owners about outstanding bills or the local farmer who paid for only two rows of weeding when he owed for three. People seemed afraid to take control of their own thinking. They allowed themselves to be manipulated. This way of life also caused me to wonder how and where I would fit in. In many ways, I remained a kind of misfit. One thing was certain: No one could chip away my self-confidence to the point of manipulating me.

I was a light-skinned person until I became stricken with a hereditary pigmentation disorder passed on from Mumma's side of the family. When I reached my early fifties, this pigmentation problem began. The first sign was dark spots like freckles on my cheeks. These spots grew bigger and bigger until they formed a dark mask over my face; at present, this disorder affects my neck, arms, and hands in the same manner. Since my colour change, those of my race who had referred to me as yellow face and half-breed now see me as odd and funny, leaving me puzzled as to whether I have moved up or dropped back a step in the black community.

As late as the 1960s, some Halifax hospitals practised social segregation. Although most black women had their babies at home with the helping hand of a midwife, a few went to the Grace Maternity Hospital. When my son Wendell was born at the Grace, two nurses wheeled me on a stretcher to the public ward following my delivery. Entering the room, one nurse started to pull the stretcher towards a bed behind the door. The other nurse said, "We won't put her there," and they put me in a bed by the window. Shortly after my arrival, a white woman was put into one of the empty centre-aisle beds. Sometime during the night I heard the nurses bringing in another woman; the next morning another black woman was in the room, this time in the bed behind the door. When John visited me that evening, he leaned over my bed by the window and laughingly asked me what I was doing here with the white women. I knew right away what he meant. I don't remember if I was placed in a bed behind a door when Miles, Cordell, and Tina were born in the same hospital, but whenever I visited black patients in a hospital, I found their beds tucked away. I used to think to myself, "Are these real cases of out of sight out of mind?" and I wondered how long it would take for our society to rid itself completely of racism, by far the worst remnant of slavery.

Slavery began to decline in Canada at the end of the eighteenth century. On June 19, 1793, a bill prohibiting the importation of slaves to Upper Canada was passed in Upper Canada's Legislative Assembly. Promoted by abolitionist Colonel John Graves Simcoe, Lieutenant Governor of Upper Canada, drafted by Chief Justice Osgoode, and introduced to the Legislative Assembly by Attorney General White, the bill declared that runaway slaves who reached Canada would be free. It did not, however, go so far as to abolish slavery within Upper Canada. Slaves were still considered the property of their owners. If a slave women had a child, that child was to be set free at the age of twenty-five. However, if a free black married a slave, their children were considered slaves.

In Nova Scotia, although some slave holders released their slaves, perhaps due to the unforeseen expenses of holding slaves in the province or to the turn of the times, others continued to maintain their slaves. In 1798, Jeremiah Northrup offered a reward through the *Royal Gazette* to any person who would return to Mr. David Rudolph at Halifax, or to himself at Falmouth, "a Negro boy . . . a smart likely lad." The deed of the sale of a slave at Windsor in 1779 testifies that a Negro slave named Mintur was sold by Joseph Northrup, of Falmouth, to John Palmer, of Windsor for "one hundred Pounds."

Black people's hatred of slavery and the determination of many people, black and white, to fight against its injustice gave birth to an organized system for harbouring and helping escaped slaves—the Underground Railroad. Beginning in the early 1800s and continuing until 1865, this network of people, many of them Quakers, worked in secret to help runaway slaves on their dangerous and frightening journey to freedom. Through rumours on the plantations, slaves learnt about station agents (called "conductors") who would hide runaway slaves (called "parcels" or "freight") and direct them to the next safe station. Risking discovery and capture along swampy, mountainous and forested paths, crossing rivers, and travelling mostly at night, the slaves made their way. Fleeing slaves from Kentucky and Virginia used a system of secret lantern signals to find underground stations—barns, cellars, and attics—that would give them safe passage into Ohio and Illinois. Levi Coffin was a famous Quaker agent who, with his wife, Catherine, helped over two thousand slaves find their way to freedom. His great work earned him the title of president of the Underground Railroad. Some abolitionists provided money to pay boat operators and wagon drivers. The fleeing runaways travelled on foot and by Great Lakes steamers, sailboats, and other floating craft to such shores as St. Catharines, Toronto, Windsor, and Montreal, later making their way in large numbers to settlements in New Brunswick and Nova Scotia.

For the hundreds of Blacks who came to Canada on the Underground Railroad, the feeling that their new environment in the north was a genuinely friendly and open atmosphere was strong. They sang slave songs such as this one during the journey to their new land:

> I'm on my way to Canada,
> That cold and dreary land;
> The dire effects of slavery,
> I can no longer stand . . .
> Farewell, old master,
> Don't come after me,
> I'm on my way to Canada
> Where coloured men are free.

Another slave wrote in the 1850s:

> Far better to breathe Canadian air
> Where all are free and well,
> Than live in slavery's atmosphere
> And wear the chains of hell.

More significant changes in the slavery laws occurred in the nine-teenth century. In 1819, after more than one thousand slaves had passed into Canada on the Underground Railroad, Attorney General John Beverley Robinson stated that with residence in Canada, Blacks were free. However, he was referring only to Blacks escaping from the United States who reached Canada; the law still did not apply to slaves already living in Canada. By this time, there was a growing anti-slavery sentiment in Canada, and more and more slaves were gaining their freedom. Nevertheless, advertisements for slaves continued to appear in newspapers as late as 1820, as in the ad for the sale of a black servant man who "is a good plain cook, understands family work and the care of horses." In 1826, Henry Clay, United States Secretary of State, asked the Canadian government for help in the return of slaves who had escaped to Canada. The Canadian govern-ment refused to help and shortly after the slave law in Canada changed. In 1833, all black people in Canada finally became free under an act passed in the British House of Commons, which abolished slavery in all of its colonies.

In 1850, the Fugitive Slave Bill was passed in the United States, giving slave-owners of the South the right to pursue and capture escaped slaves living in the free northern states. For black people the new bill was an ominous threat to their newly gained freedom. During this time hundreds more fled across the border into Canada through the Underground Railroad. In 1850, the total population of Blacks in Nova Scotia was close to 4,900. Ten years later, as a result of the Fugitive Slave Bill, the population had increased to 6,000. If caught helping fugitive slaves people could be punished with huge fines, hand branding with the letters "SS" (slave stealer), or impris-onment. These threats, however, did not dampen the spirits of people such as Laura Haviland and Thomas Garrett, who had been helping slaves since 1786. In 1848, Garret assisted in transporting a free slave and his family from Delaware to Philadelphia. Despite the court damages this good deed cost him, he continued to help.

Another abolitionist undaunted by the Fugitive Slave Bill was Harriet Tubman, the woman called Moses and the most famous conductor on the Underground Railroad. Born a slave at Dorchester County, Maryland in 1820 or 1821, Harriet Tubman escaped to Philadelphia in 1849. For the next two years she made several trips back to Maryland and helped bring some of her family and other slaves to Philadelphia. During one of her trips in 1851, she realized she had to guide the slaves beyond Philadelphia to assure their safety, so she returned to Maryland for a group of eleven slaves, then set out for Canada. At least one stationmaster refused to help her because there were too many, but with the help of Frederick and Anne Douglas, whose home in Rochester, New York was an "overflow station," Harriet and her group arrived in St. Catharines in late December 1851. Concerning this particular trip, Frederick Douglas is known to have stated, "It was difficult for us to give shelter, food and money for so many at once, but it had to be done so they could be moved on immediately to Canada." This group of eleven included one of Harriet's brothers and his wife. Harriet Tubman continued to risk being recaptured as she conducted more than three hundred slaves to freedom while the price on her own head soared. She died on March 10, 1913, as her friends joined hands and sang her beloved song, "Swing Low Sweet Chariot." Another well-known black stationmaster of the Underground Railroad was Garmain Wesley Loguen, a one-time slave who escaped to Canada and is credited with helping about 1,500 other slaves do the same. He was a close friend of Harriet Tubman and was known as the Underground Railroad King.

In the early 1850s, a white abolitionist from Kansas, John Brown, came to Chatham (Ontario) to plan a military strategy to dismantle the slave system. Brown gathered together a group of men to wage guerrilla warfare, outlining a plan to attack the American arsenal at Harpers Ferry, West Virginia. He would arm his followers and march south, smashing slavery and setting up a provisional government of the United States. After learning that a traitor had leaked news of the Chatham meeting to American authorities, the attack was postponed until October 16, 1859. It was a major incident in the long struggle over slavery in the United States. Of the twenty-one men involved in the attempted overthrow, ten were killed, six escaped, and five were later hanged. John Brown was tried on October 31, 1859 for first degree murder and conspiracy with slaves to rebel. He was found guilty and hanged in Charleston, West Virginia on December 2, 1859. Osborne Perry Anderson, a black Canadian, was one of the few that escaped death or capture at Harpers Ferry. He returned to Canada with the help of the Underground Railroad and wrote about his experiences in the book *A Voice from Harpers Ferry*. The attack on Harpers Ferry made a great impression on Canadians and still has them singing the song, "John Brown's body lies a-mouldering in the grave. His truth goes marching on." During the American Civil War (1861-1865), the Union troops sang this song as they marched south to fight against slavery.

American Congress abolished slavery on April 16, 1863, by which time some forty thousand black fugitives had entered Canada. Slaves who fled across the border on the Underground Railroad and made their way to Nova Scotia found freedom, but only a freedom of sorts, for the racism that fuelled slavery and allowed for its cruelty continued long after ex-slaves and their children settled in Nova Scotia and started building their own communities.

Despite the dramatic increase of the black presence in Canada since the arrival of Mathieu da Costa in the first years of the seventeenth century, and despite the collapse of institutional slavery, deep-rooted prejudices by whites continued to stand as a roadblock to freedom and equality for all Blacks in Canada. Religion, a powerful force that had given Loyalist settlers, refugees, and slaves hope during their most difficult times became ever more important to this demoralized group as they attempted to develop the communities they had dreamed of. Then, as now, building community meant getting involved in church life.

When white Loyalists first arrived in Nova Scotia, they organized Methodist, Anglican, Baptist, Presbyterian, and Roman Catholic churches in the areas they settled. However, when the black Loyalists arrived in Nova Scotia between 1782 and 1784, they discovered that the existing churches would only receive them as "special" members—with separate seating and facilities. Eventually, like in the United States where Blacks were not allowed to attend white

Methodist churches, most churches advised black church members to find their own meeting place. Disappointed in the attitudes and behaviour of their white neighbours, most Blacks did turn back to their own communities for religious instruction and practice. Thus was born the African Methodist Movement in Nova Scotia.

By 1784, one quarter of Nova Scotia's Methodists were black. John Wesley, the Methodist founder, vowed to keep black Methodists supplied with religious books and encouraged white Methodists to give them assistance. In 1784, many of the free black Loyalists living in Birchtown established the first independent black church, the African Methodist Episcopal, under the ministry of Moses Wilkinson, a blind, former slave and Methodist preacher. Moses Wilkinson had sailed from New York to Port Roseway (Shelburne), Nova Scotia in 1753. He was a member of the Black Pioneers Corps and lived in Birchtown.

As Reverend Wilkinson's congregation increased, he began to inspire a black Loyalist named Boston King to take up the ministry. King had run away from his master in South Carolina and went to New York. He was recaptured there and placed under armed guard close to the Hudson River. Early one Sunday morning he crept quietly to the river and disappeared into the mist before the guards awoke to catch him. Having swum some distance from the shore, he proceeded forward through bushes and marsh near the road. There he found a boat, which he used to get to Canada. Reverend King's preaching took him from the Shelburne district to Digby, Halifax, and Preston. In 1791, Reverend King was placed in charge of a Methodist group in Preston. In his autobiography, King wrote about the problems facing poor black people: "Many of the poor people were compelled to sell their best gown for five pounds of flour, in order to support life. When they were parted with all their clothes, even their blankets, several of them fell down dead in the streets through hunger. Some killed and ate their dog and cat; and poverty and distress prevailed on every side."

Reverend Joshua Wingate Weeks, the white Anglican clergyman from St. Paul's Church in Halifax, began travelling to Preston to minister to the settlers there, and the Anglican church was soon after

invisible shadows

established in Preston. Some black people of Preston went to the recently consecrated white Anglican church because they wanted to attend a church in their own community. Although governmental authorities felt uncertain that the poor white and black communities of Preston could support a church, Governor Parr finally decided in 1787 to allow a church to be built. The Legislature granted Anglican Bishop Inglis a sum of money to be used in building the church, a sum the bishop issued in three lots. The first amount was issued when the contract with the workmen was made. The second was issued on April 7, 1789, when the frame was boarded in and the roof was shingled. The third sum of money was issued on January 30, 1790, when the windows and doors were installed, the walls plastered, and the pews put in place. This new church was erected on a one-acre parcel of land on Crane Hill in an area populated by black Loyalists. The acre of land containing the church and graveyard on Crane Hill was donated to the Church of England by a dissenting Protestant of Preston, believed to have been Theophilus Chamberlain.

This church, called St. John's-on-the-Hill, and the cemetery next to the church were consecrated by Bishop Inglis on June 26, 1791. Most black people only worshipped there for a short period of time, then began to have services in private Preston homes, such as that of the black school teacher, Mrs. Catherine Abernathy. In the winter of 1822, St. John's Church on Crane Hill collapsed. The church, which became known as St. John's Anglican Church, was rebuilt in 1828 on the base-ball diamond near William Ross School on the Number Seven Highway, just outside of the black community of Preston. A forest fire in June 1849 destroyed that church and the third St. John's Church was consecrated in 1851 at its present location on the corner of Lake Major Road and the Number Seven Highway.

Around this time the Baptist religion was also gaining in popular-ity in the black settlements of Nova Scotia. David George, one of the founders of the first black church in America in 1773, the Silver Bluff Baptist Church in South Carolina, is credited with starting Baptist church work in Preston. He left to preach in Birchtown, the black set-tlement at Shelburne, but returned to Preston in 1791.

Although David George was only in Preston for a short time, he became popular among black and white settlers alike. Some of Reverend Weeks' followers were drawn to George's fiery evangelistic preaching and changed ministers. George converted and baptized five people—whites and blacks both—and started a Baptist congregation in Preston, which he placed under the leadership of one of his assistants, Hector Peters. David George continued his house-to-house preaching and his baptizing until January 15, 1792, when he joined Reverend Moses Wilkinson, Reverend Boston King, and the 1,200 Blacks who immigrated to Sierra Leone, Africa. Upon their arrival in Sierra Leone, the group ceremoniously planted a bag of soil from Nova Scotia. The Sierra Leone exodus took some of the most prominent black preachers, teachers and leaders, leaving black Baptist and Methodist churches in Nova Scotia somewhat quiet for a time.

In 1795, John Burton took up the work started by David George. Burton was a white Episcopalian missionary from Durham, England, known to the black people as Father Burton. He came to Halifax on May 20, 1792, and in 1793 he visited the United States, where he became a Baptist. In 1795, he established the first Baptist church in Halifax on the south-east corner of Barrington and Buckingham streets. Known as Burton's Church, its congregation totalled thirty-three and was composed mainly of black people, some of them early Loyalists. Baptists left behind by David George in 1792 also joined this church and membership increased again as black refugees began arriving in Halifax following the war of 1812. By 1820, the congregation in Burton's church had increased by approximately three hundred members. Membership increased again in 1824, when dissension among the leaders of St. Paul's Church resulted in a schism and a group of Anglicans called "dissenters" joined Burton's Church and became Baptists. The leader of this group, Robert Davis, a preacher from Lunenburg, felt uneasy worshipping with black people so he tried to rid Burton's church of its black members. But the black people maintained their respect for John Burton and stayed at his church. Eventually, Davis and the "dissenters" left Father Burton's church and established a Baptist church of their own.

The civil authorities gave Father Burton responsibility for the black people in Preston, Dartmouth, Cherry Brook, Lake Loon, Musquodoboit Road, Fall River, Beech Hill (Beechville), Hammonds Plains, and Campbell Road (Africville), while he was their pastor. It was in all these black settlements that Father Burton preached, baptized, married and buried. He continued work among the black Baptists until he recognized the leadership qualities of one of his black church members, Richard Preston. Preston had arrived in Nova Scotia from Virginia in 1815 in search of his mother, who he learnt had come to Canada. Not realizing Canada was so large, he intended to search from east to west. Upon entering the port in Halifax, he learnt of a black settlement called Preston and thought to start his search there. Near the corner of the Old Preston Road and Brian Road, he came to a hut and enquired of an elderly lady about his mother. As the lady was about to close the door on him, she raised her lantern and saw a scar on the stranger's neck. It was this scar that united that mother to her long lost son. After all hopes of ever seeing him again had passed from her memory, it was like a miracle that he found her in a black settlement bearing his name.

Father Burton encouraged the Baptists in Halifax to send Preston to England to be educated for the ministry. Preston landed at Liverpool, England on February 15, 1831. The West London Association of Baptist Ministers formed a committee to give direction to brother Preston during his studies, and on May 18, 1832 he was ordained in London, England at the Grafton Street Chapel. The London Baptists gave Father Preston 630 pounds for the purchase of land and the erection of a church, and the African Baptist mother church was built on Cornwallis Street in Halifax in 1832. The transition of black Baptists from Burton's church to Cornwallis Street Church was orderly. Father Burton gave Father Preston much information and assistance. They travelled throughout the province and in each county where black people assembled, they appointed an elder. Father Burton eventually handed the charges of those little village assemblies over to Father Preston. John Burton died February 6, 1838.

Father Preston's personal witnessing and ministry appealed to the people who had been cast away by the Anglican church and under his guidance they rallied to the Baptist cause. He organized the First Preston Church in 1842, and went on to organize other churches all connected to the Cornwallis Street Baptist Church in Halifax, including Dartmouth Lake Church, Beech Hill and Cherry Brook Churches (1844), Hammonds Plains Church (1845), Campbell Road (1849), Bear River, Digby, Weymouth Falls, Greenville, and Bridgetown churches (1853). During Father Preston's ministry, as with the ministry of past and future black preachers, he not only handled the affairs of the church but also of the community. He worked very closely with government officials as he endeavoured to solve the numerous problems confronting black people. Petitions were constantly being made to the government on behalf of the sick and the poor as well as for additional land.

All was well in the congregation of Preston Church until 1856, when dissension caused some members to leave the church and organize their own. Between 1840 and 1860, Father Preston had been taking one of the original members of Preston's Baptist church, James Thomas, with him on his ministry throughout the province. Although Thomas was white, he became an original member of Cornwallis Street Baptist Church. The Thomases were strict Welsh Baptists, which made it quite easy for their son James to begin his Baptist church work amongst black Baptists such as John Burton and Richard Preston. Preston and Thomas often journeyed on foot from Halifax to Yarmouth, stopping to hold meetings in all the little black churches along the way.

Father Preston ordained James Thomas in 1857. Thomas married Hannah Saunders, a black woman, and they lived and raised their family on a large farm located between East and North Preston. Thomas eventually succeeded Father Preston as pastor of the Preston Church, but was faced with the same dissension amongst his congregation in Preston that Father Preston had faced. Conflict at Preston Church increased and in 1869 Reverend James Thomas left the pastorate to be replaced by Reverend George Neale.

Born in Georgia in 1807, baptized in 1815 by Father Burton, and ordained by Father Thomas in 1864, Father Neale was very pleased to have young folks come into the congregation, referring to them as the lambs of the fold. When Father Preston's congregation became divided in 1856, those who left organized a new church known as South Church. Pastored by Benson Smithers until 1867, it was located on what is known as upper Governor Street today. Just before Thomas's death in 1879, Father Neale organized the scattered members of South Preston Church into a body on the New Road settlement. These members constructed a new church building, which they named Saint Thomas Baptist Church, although it was also known as New Road Church.

Father Preston called together representatives from twelve black churches in Nova Scotia; at this meeting at Granville Mountain on September 1, 1854, the African United Baptist Association (AUBA) of Nova Scotia was organized. Reverend Thomas succeeded Preston as moderator of the AUBA and served from 1861 to 1879. When

Cornwallis Street Baptist Church is known as the "Mother Church" to Nova Scotia's black Baptists.

Reverend Thomas left the pastorate at Preston Church in 1869, the church left the AUBA, but returned under the leadership of Reverend George Neale in 1890. That Reverend Thomas was a white man who wanted authority over this black organization did not sit well with Reverend Benson Smithers, pastor of South Church, or with his congregation in Preston. This conflict ended with Reverend Thomas remaining as moderator, and Smithers and eleven of his supporters being found guilty of indecent conduct. Smithers' clergyman credentials were annulled and he and his eleven followers were expelled from membership in the African United Baptist Association.

In 1874, George Carvery, a member of Preston Church, was ordained and that same year, he, like Reverend Thomas, broke away from Preston Church and organized the Fulton Church on Frog Lake Road. Reverend Neale remained pastor at First Preston Church until 1893, when Reverend Edward Dixon replaced him. Dixon lived in Africville and walked over fifteen miles to Preston on the weekends to serve the congregation. Reverend John Smith succeeded Dixon following Dixon's death in 1908. In 1910, shortly after Smith succumbed to illness, Preston church was turned over to a young man, Arthur A. Wyse from Lake Loon, who had been working in the recently organized Cherry Brook Church. The first church I ever attended outside of our church in Mount Denson was the one in Cherry Brook. and Arthur Wyse was the first pastor I came to know in Preston. Preston's new church building was erected in 1917. It became known as East Preston United Baptist Church (rather than First Preston Church). The Preston church congregation honoured and loved Reverend Wyse's ministry and he remained pastor of East Preston United Baptist Church until 1953—the longest serving pastorate in one church in the AUBA.

I knew that attending church would help me grow into my new community, and I slowly became accustomed to the style of worship carried on at East Preston United Baptist Church, where I was greeted by an usher's warm, friendly smile each time I entered. The elderly women would mother me and approach me after the service saying, "Girl, when are you going to join us." Their question was answered on July 12, 1959, the day I became a member of their congregation.

It should be remembered that a relaxed lifestyle was very much a part of the character of the community during the 1950s. During this time, church affairs were still in the hands of the men. Women were considered helpmates and their duties were to assist in carrying out the church's work. Young people were to observe and learn from their elders, who reprimanded and taught not only their own children but other children as well. All church members were considered a part of God's family and so referred to each other as "brother" and "sister." The church brothers belonged to the group known as "The Brotherhood," and held their meetings in the church. The sisters' group was called the "Ladies Auxiliary" and they held monthly meetings in their homes.

When I was baptized and joined the church, the congregation made me feel like a part of their family. I found church members had deeply ingrained religious beliefs and some rigid standards. The congregation bonded like a family. There were times I found myself sharing things with my church sisters that I had not shared with my biological sisters.

The Reverend Donald Skier came to Preston Church in 1953; over the course of his ministry he married, buried, christened and bap-

The East Preston Baptist Church (at left). Community residents gathered at church on Sundays to the clear, joyous sound of the church bell chiming.

tized many of the community's residents. He performed Preston's largest baptism—110 people—in July 1976 in Partridge River. Pastor Skier lived in Halifax and served as pastor at New Road (North Preston) and Cherry Brook churches also. A member of one of these congregations picked him up and drove him to Sunday services, church meetings, and community functions. Every Sunday he preached one service in each of these churches.

The second Sunday in October was Harvest Sunday—a special service where the farmers used the pretty fall leaves to decorate baskets of fruit and vegetables that had been gathered in the harvest and brought to the church. During the service, prayers of thanks were given. The next day, "Thanksgiving Day," all the baskets of fruit and vegetables were taken from the church to Partridge River School, where in the evening they were auctioned off to raise funds for the church. Before the auction began, some of the harvest was delivered to the community elders, widows, the sick, and the shut-in. Many residents from the surrounding black communities attended the Harvest Sunday service and joined us in our homes for a tasty harvest dinner.

Christmas was also a special time in the church and the community. The Ladies Auxiliary held a special service in the church and a Christmas Tea and Sale in the Partridge River School. The newly formed Women's Missionary Society made up Christmas cheer baskets of fruit and candy. It was during this season that everyone went from home to home, enjoying a piece of Christmas cake with a cup of hot tea or a glass of home-made wine. The church watch service was held on New Year's Eve. Even before reaching the church, we could hear the congregation singing Christmas carols. Everyone arrived at the church to await midnight, at which time everyone knelt and gave thanks to God for allowing them to see another old year out and a new year in.

These traditions created and kept a community bond in Preston. During choir practice and at every church service the organist played and directed the choir. The church clerk kept records of all church business. The deacons put in endless hours, leading services, visiting homes throughout the community, and assisting the church pastor. Every spring and fall, a small group of women from the church soci-

invisible shadows

eties would take their mops, pails, and cleaning supplies and give the church a good cleaning. Church handy men like Charles Colley came out and made repairs around the church. Many hands made these duties easy, but, unlike today, asking payment for such services was unthinkable. Indeed, it was the unpaid labour of church members such as William B. Thomas, Florence Diggs, Charles Colley, Florence James, Fred Riley, Elsie Johnston, and others that kept dedicated service alive in our church.

In the summer, the second Sunday of July was a special day in the church known as "Baptism Sunday." Preston Church did not have a baptismal pool, so the ceremony took place in the Partridge River. During this sacred time, a person wanting to make a spiritual transition went to a secluded place in or around their home for a period of quietude and preparation. Those being baptized were called candidates. Vivid in my mind is the baptism Sunday of July 12, 1959, when I was one of the twenty-nine candidates. We were dressed in white baptismal gowns, white headpieces, white gloves, and white sneakers. As we lined up behind the minister and deacons in a double line, one line for the women and another for the men, Deacon Evans took me to the front to lead the women and Lawrence Saunders to lead the men. The choir lined up behind the candidates, followed by the congregation. What a splendid sight to see the minister lead the procession from the church to Partridge River, while the choir sang such old-time Negro spirituals as, "Take Me to The Water to Be Baptized," "Hallelujah 'Tis Done I Believe on the Son," and "Satan Is Mad and I Am Glad He Missed the Soul He Thought He Had." As they stood on the river bank, the whole congregation joined in the singing while a deacon led the candidates one by one into the water. The singing stopped each time the minister asked a candidate "Do you take Jesus as your personal Lord and Saviour?" As the candidate was led out of the water, the singing began again.

After we were baptized, we went home to remove our wet clothes. My mother was with me and she had my dry clothes laid out for me when I got home. Once changed, I returned to church to receive the "right hand of fellowship," which meant I was now a member of the church. During this service of worship, the old spirituals were once again sung to the tune of the organ. As I write this, I can almost hear Grandma Crawley singing, "There's going to be a meeting in the air. In the sweet by and by and all my friends will meet me over there way-up in the sky." That day, as I stood at the river bank and viewed the marvellous scene, my imagination drew a picture of the baptism which took place in Jordan River, when John the Baptist baptized Jesus (St. Matthew:3).

Following my baptism, I had a desire to get involved with the women who were doing things in the church, the group of women called the "Ladies Auxiliary." Conceived on September 3, 1917 at the African United Baptist Association (AUBA) session at East Preston, the Ladies Auxiliary came to life under the guidance of Mrs. C.S. McLearn of the Baptist Convention Women's Missionary Union, who had been

River baptism in the black church of Nova Scotia goes back to the days of David George. In 1783, a few days before his first Christmas in Shelburne, he broke the ice in his creek and baptized his first four candidates.

invisible shadows

invited to the meeting to assist the women in organizing just such a group. Mrs. McLearn and twenty-one black women from Nova Scotia gathered around a well near East Preston Baptist Church. Following Mrs. McLearn's talk, the women envisioned home mission work they could carry out in their local churches to promote and sustain the spiritual and cultural levels of all African Baptist women. Sister Bessie Wyse, wife of Preston's pastor, was elected official organizer of the Ladies Auxiliary of the African United Baptist Association. Their first officers were inducted: President Sister Maude Sparks; Vice-Presidents, Sisters Jane Hamilton, Rufus Marsman, Martha Middleton, Margaret Upshaw, and Julia Williams; Secretary, Sister Rachel Upshaw; Assistant Secretary, Sister Sarah Clayton; Treasurer, Sister Louisa Bundy.

Word about the meeting at the well spread throughout Nova Scotia's AUBA churches and the vision of all church women becoming helpers began to catch on. One year later, in September 1918, AUBA official organizer Sister Bessie Wyse organized twenty-four ladies at East Preston Baptist Church into a Ladies Auxiliary, at which time these ladies elected their first slate of officers: President, Sister Isabel Diggs; Vice-president, Sister Maggie Williams; Secretary, Sister Sarah Clayton; Assistant Secretary, Sister Annie Thomas; and Treasurer, Sister Nancy Colley. Possessed with limited education and struggling against traditional opposition to women taking on leadership roles, members of the Ladies Auxiliary continued to make it clear that there was a place for their witness and work within the church. The Ladies Auxiliary was the first organized society in East Preston Baptist Church.

A few times after church service, Deacon Evans approached me to say, "Sister, I am expecting great things from you, as many come but only few are called." I never forgot these words, which helped to inspire me to become more active in the church. When sisters Jean Evans, Florence Diggs, Mable Saunders, Marjorie Ross, Freda Williams, and Wilhelmina Riley wanted me to join the Ladies Auxiliary, it didn't take much encouragement. The Ladies Auxiliary meetings were held the third Tuesday afternoon of each month at a different member's home. It was at the meeting of July 19, 1960 at the home of Sister Lavinia Glasgow that I joined the Ladies Auxiliary.

The meeting opened with the president reading the scripture lesson taken from John, chapter fourteen, followed by prayers. This was an annual meeting where all the committee reports were read and officers re-elected for the next year. Following the business session, the meeting adjourned and the sisters formed a circle, joining hands and repeating the mizpah—"the Lord watch between me and thee, when we are absent one from the other. Amen." We then enjoyed the beautiful meal sister Glasgow had prepared for the group of fourteen. I enjoyed every minute of our fellowship hour. The older sisters told stories about past happenings in the Ladies Auxiliary. They also gave the younger sisters tips on raising a family and on home remedies. I met sister Cecilia Brown, one of Preston's midwives. She told me she knew when a woman was pregnant by looking into her eyes.

Each month I learnt something new from these sisters. I appreciated the experience I gained from cooking and helping prepare for the special fund-raising dinners and other functions. Many times the sisters chose me as their speaker at regular and special occasion church services. This often included speaking at other AUBA churches in the province. I held the office of president from 1985 to 1987 and compiled a brief history ("The Meeting at the Well") for our sixty-ninth Ladies Auxiliary Anniversary.

The Ladies Auxiliary carried out a variety of church duties, including helping the janitor. When I joined the church, it had a woodburning furnace and sometimes during winter the church was so hot one could smell the heat, and at other times it was so cold it would cause goose pimples. There was one man, Brother Harris Brown, who made a special effort to start the furnace in plenty of time to warm the church up before service began. When Brother Howard Williams took over the janitor job, he kept the fires burning in the furnace. However, the furnace made for a lot of smoke and sooty dust, which had to be washed off the walls, pews, and everything. The church janitor was paid little or nothing for his services, so the ladies lent a helping hand. Twice a year four or five of us took our cleaning equipment and supplies to the church and performed a general house cleaning.

During one clean-up day, a couple of us thought it would be nice if the church had an oil furnace. We took our idea to the auxiliary meeting; the ladies agreed, and the church' s first oil furnace was installed. It is important to add that this addition did not mean that Brother Howard spent any less time working. He was dedicated to his job and kept the church nice and clean. The hymnals were always neatly stacked at the back of the church and the pews well dusted. It was a pleasure walking into a nice, clean, warm church.

Raising funds to make the monthly payments on the oil furnace was done by holding concerts, bake sales, giggs dinner, or bean supper in Partridge River School. Sometimes we held a corn boil or wiener roast in Sister Riley's backyard. Raffles and punch cards were good fund-raisers too. Payments were always made on time, which kept the sisters busy. The Ladies Auxiliary also worked together to study problems of home improvement, education, and employment in much the same way as the women who began the organization.

Truly enjoying the warm, relaxed atmosphere and the friendly hospitality, and being a relatively new member, I was afraid to ask a

East Preston Ladies Auxiliary, 1987. I'm sixth from the left in the front row. At an auxiliary meeting held on October 28, 1955, a motion passed that all sisters wear black skirts, white blouses and black hats for all auxiliary programs.

question that nagged at me: why did the men meet in the church and women in their homes? However, when curiosity finally got the best of me, I questioned the older auxiliary members and started reading old church minutes and a brief church history to find an answer. After discovering that since 1918 the women's group had been meeting in their homes, I started thinking that meetings should be moved to the church. When I heard Sister Mildred Law, a missionary from India, speak at the Ladies Auxiliary session of the AUBA on August 22, 1960, I felt the need to get involved in mission outreach. I mentioned the concern to Sister Pearleen Oliver, and she told me of the work being carried on by the United Baptist Women's Missionary Union of the Maritime Provinces made up of Women's Missionary Societies (WMS). When our Ladies Auxiliary members heard of the WMS, they too became interested.

In 1961, Sister Pearleen Oliver and a member of the United Baptist Missionary Union were invited to East Preston Baptist Church to organize a group of eighteen women into a Women's Missionary Society. Their first official slate of officers was elected: President, Sister Verna Thomas; Vice-president, Sister Ada Williams; Secretary, Sister Marguerite Thomas; and Treasurer, Sister Edith Colley. Monthly meetings of the WMS were held in the church. At last, one group of women was meeting in the church! It was at this time that membership in the Ladies Auxiliary had increased to the point that meetings had to be moved to the church as well. The auxiliary's last meeting outside the church was held at the home of Sister Lillian Colley on December 12, 1961. The first monthly meeting in the church took place on January 16, 1962.

The WMS endeavoured to send out and maintain women missionaries, teachers, and other helpers in foreign fields as well as in Canada. Our Preston group made contributions of canned and dried foods and small funds to a foreign mission, purchased yearly tidings, held prayer services in the homes of the elders and sick in the community, participated in the World Day of Prayer every March, periodically had special church services in our church, and sent a delegate from our group to the United Baptist Women's Missionary Union's annual convention. The convention was holding their fifty-sixth annual meeting at Acadia University, Wolfville from August 28 to September 3, 1962, when our group was organized. The first delegates to go from our Preston group were Sister Mable Saunders and myself. Most of the fund-raising for our trip was done through tea and sales at the Partridge River School, though we also collected a good amount when I thought up the travelling apron idea. Each month, an apron with many small pockets on it was given to a member of the group to wear around her kitchen. People coming in were encouraged to put some money into one of the pockets. Most ladies brought it back with money in every pocket. I made this apron from a yard of printed cotton purchased from Simpson's catalogue.

During the month of July and August, the group didn't hold meetings, so in May each member took home a small pasteboard mite box for family or friends who stopped by to drop a few pennies, nickels, or dimes into. These boxes were taken back at the September meeting, the money was counted, then turned over for foreign mission work. We also sent food parcels to the missionaries in Africa.

In the province's early history, when the government did not feel that education was its concern, it was black people's belief that education could solve many of their problems. However, in the areas throughout the province where schools existed, black children were excluded from attending just as they and their families had been excluded from white churches. Before organized education began in 1796, Blacks remained functionally illiterate, although some received basic education through the church. Church leaders saw the effect illiteracy was having on black people and recognized the need for schools in the community, and so the segregated school system was established.

The black Loyalists received funds in 1785 from the associates of the late Dr. Bray and a charitable Anglican organization known as "The Society for the Propagation of the Gospel (SPG)" to start a school in Preston. Their efforts were centred in the Maritimes with Preston's school being one of the first five schools it founded. The community's church leaders, although barely literate, became the pioneer teachers. David George, Boston King, and Isaac Limerick along with Catherine Abernathy taught twenty children in the one-room log schoolhouse. Reverend Joshua Wingate Weeks, the Anglican minister from St. Paul's Church who had been ministering to the Anglicans of Preston since 1785, became concerned about the school's standards. He wrote to the SPG about the education of Blacks, and asked if the school could be upgraded to match the standards of other such schools. The SPG agreed and financial support was granted on the condition that Weeks inspect the school to insure that teachers were giving what the Anglican church considered "proper training." This first school in Preston remained open until 1792, when its teachers joined the mass exodus of black Loyalists, under the leadership of Thomas Peters and David George, to Sierra Leone.

With the coming of the Jamaican Maroons in 1796 the issue of education was revisited. Reverend Benjamin Gray, an Anglican missionary to the Maroons in Preston, constructed a school in 1797 and taught the Maroon children. Again the SPG assisted and in the spring of 1799 three dozen Dixon spelling books arrived. One year later, in August 1800, the discontented Maroons left Nova Scotia for Sierra Leone, and Preston's school doors closed once again.

In 1811, the Education Act was passed, ensuring that any district in the province with thirty families or more that could build a school, hire a teacher, and come up with fifty to two hundred pounds sterling would receive a government subsidy. Since black communities could not meet these requirements, the only education black children received was that sponsored by the Society of the Propagation of the Gospel, and the few black schools this society did maintain came to an end in the mid-nineteenth century.

In 1876 all black children were excluded from public white schools if a black school existed in their area. The black schools established by school inspectors were truly inferior to other schools in terms of staff and facilities—the communities simply did not have the funds to train adequate teachers and maintain their schools independently. However, they provided the only formal education available to black children. In 1884, special government grants were given to support private and segregated schools in Nova Scotia's black communities. Preston was one of the communities to receive such a grant. When I interviewed Myrtle Bundy in 1972, she could still recall attending the one-room log schoolhouse located across the bridge in the centre of what is now the Number Seven Highway. The school was heated by a potbelly wood stove in the middle of the classroom floor, and during winter months the students took turns sitting in front of it to get warm. Water was carried by wooden buckets from the nearest spring. The students' textbooks were cast-offs, torn and marked-up. Myrtle Bundy's first teacher was a white man, John T. Irving, but she remembered other teachers such as Mr. King, Spurgeon Paris, Gus Anderson, Mrs. Scott, Ethel Gibson, and Martha Jones. The little log school Myrtle attended came to an end in 1917, but the love for poetry she learnt there lasted throughout her life.

Poverty and oppression prevented the students from attending school regularly and very few could remain in school past an early age. Poor school attendance was a constant complaint from early school administrators. Children were kept home often during harsh winter conditions as many did not have warm clothing to wear and often during the school year when they were needed at home to assist their parents with chores. Many older children worked as domestic servants and labourers and could only attend school when they were not working. The teachers used to miss a number of days themselves.

During the 1920s, a one-room school was built at Brian Street, just across the road from Partridge River. About thirty children attended this school. Like the log school, it was segregated and kept Preston children at a disadvantage with its poor facilities. As late as 1940, many teachers who taught at Partridge River School weren't educated beyond grade ten. Under these circumstances, students' chances of becoming university educated were slim. However, it was at Partridge River School that the first black teaching graduate taught; Madeline Francis-Symonds graduated from the Provincial Normal School (later known as the Nova Scotia Teacher's College) in 1928. Although most of her teaching years were spent at Upper Hammonds Plains School, in 1940 she taught a half term at the Partridge River School. Like in the early part of the century, poor attendance kept children below their grade level. Children in primary and grade one didn't know their colours; grade two and three students didn't know their ABCs.

Preston children continued to endure the poor facilities in their little one-room segregated school until 1945 when the government granted a one thousand-acre wood lot to each the church and the school, from which wood and timber could be sold. But the old school's trustees could neither read nor write, so when they were approached by a white lumberjack, Ginger Smith, concerning land, they took him at his word and signed his papers. It turned out that they had signed the school and church wood lot over to Ginger Smith. Upon learning how the trustees had been conned, the people appointed new ones. One of the new trustees appointed in 1945 was James Slawter, who remained a member of the Partridge River School Board for twenty-nine years.

The new board of trustees had the one-room school torn down and a new two-room school built in 1945 on the same location. The new school had tables and benches for desks and a coal and wood stove for heat. Although this was only a two-room school, it meant a lot to community residents. They held a big opening dance in the Eastern Star Lodge Hall on Brian Street to celebrate. Dorothy Ewing-Williams recalls her studies at Partridge River School, where about fifty children attended grades primary to eight. The older students went in the morning and the primary children in the afternoon. Although this was a black school, a few white children from the surrounding white neighbourhood attended. Dorothy remembers the school was sometimes quite cold and uncomfortable. The boys had to go outside and gather wood to help keep the classroom warm. Many students had a long way to walk to school so when the weather was bad, very few attended. The school grounds were rough and the students and staff used outdoor washrooms.

Some teachers who taught at the old Partridge River School were Arthur Morgan, Claire Jemmott, Elsa Reddick, Ms. Hill, and Inez Cromwell. Their salary ranged from two to three hundred dollars a year—whatever was raised by funds from concerts and door-to-door canvassing. Teachers were paid thirty to fifty dollars at Easter and Christmas, and the balance at the end of the school term in July. The government gave the school trustees a small grant at the end of the school year to help pay the balance of the teachers' salaries. It was a real task for the trustees to raise money in a community where everyone was pinching pennies themselves. The majority of students came from large families who were finding it difficult to make ends meet. Most of these students had to drop out of school to help with the raising of younger siblings or to seek employment. When these students left school, a great number of them were unable to read, write or comprehend elementary sentences.

It was clear that the black population of Nova Scotia lagged behind the majority in educational levels. Fortunately, in the late 1940s, the school trustees found an answer to the community's basic education problem in Inez Cromwell, a well trained, caring teacher, whose work resulted in improved attendance and improved interest on the part of the parents. Most importantly, the students at Partridge River School became aware of their own need for education. A breakthrough in education came when three of Inez Cromwell's students completed their studies at Partridge River School and continued on to high school. These students were Dorothy Ewing, Geneva Gray, and Leonard Diggs. Dorothy and Leonard continued their education at Hawthorn, St. Peters, and Greenfield high schools in Dartmouth, and Geneva studied further in Halifax.

In 1950, the two-room school was expanded to eleven rooms with a foundation to accommodate students from primary to grade nine. The school's curriculum then included home economics, industrial arts, and music. Five years previously, Shirley Morgan, a teacher at the Nova Scotia Home for Coloured Children, was hired by the Department of Education to organize a home economics curriculum in six black rural communities in Halifax County. Teachers travelled to the various black schools to teach weekly classes on following a recipe, setting a table, and serving food. Also in 1950, the Nova Scotia Department of Education assigned Noel Johnston to bring manual arts instruction to black schools. Johnston and the industrial arts inspector installed work benches and power tools in the empty shell of a bus and drove the equipment, machines, and materials from school to school throughout Halifax County. This mobile classroom, known as "the shopmobile," had room for eight to ten boys at a time, each with their own workstation. Students learnt how to use basic hand tools, power tools, and were also familiarized with blueprints and drafting. The boys worked on their own projects, making a birdhouse, a cutting board, or a lawn ornament.

I didn't need a calendar to tell me when home economics classes were being given at Partridge River School. This class was in frequent need of a cup of sugar, flour, raisins, or other baking ingredients. Living across the road from the school made me a prime target in the time of need, and I was never surprised (or disappointed) to see some little girl knock on my door with a cup in her hand. I also looked forward to seeing the shopmobile drive into the schoolyard. If I needed a pair of scissors or a knife sharpened, Noel was obliged to help. These two programs added a ray of hope for black children. In 1957, when the school trustees secured a new principal for Partridge River School, they engaged the well qualified and experienced H. A. J. Wedderburn, who remained in the position until 1961. The discrepancy between the number of students registered and those actually in attendance caused him concern, so he made improving school attendance his immediate goal; it was impossible, he realized, to teach a student who was absent from class. Shortly after Wedderburn's arrival, Partridge River School attendance reached an all-time high. Wedderburn's interest in the students and their own accomplishments in the home economics and shopmobile programs motivated them to do well in other school subjects.

In 1959, I became president of the Partridge River Home and School Association and in meetings with the principal and school trustees learnt of the serious problems facing students, namely poor reading skills and the lack of books and other resource materials. Aware of the Halifax County Bookmobile services, I had a feeling that this travelling library might be of benefit to Preston residents. I immediately brought this to the trustees' and the principal's attention. Both

invisible shadows

Gordie Marshall's class, Ross Road School, 1973. My son Miles is seventh from the left in the second row. After school Miles would rather feed and care for our dog than do his homework.

students and teachers were happy to have Bookmobile Number Two come once a month, with two stops in Preston: one at Partridge River school and one in my yard. Even after the school was closed, the bookmobile continued its monthly service stop in my yard until 1997.

In the early 1970s, changes began to take place in Partridge River School. Children from North Preston were no longer attending home economics classes at this school and there were no white children in attendance there. Our own children were being bussed out of the community at a very early grade to attend schools in communities like Humber Park, Cole Harbour, and Ross Road. Eventually, students from grades five to seven were bussed out of Preston to attend Ross Road School, leaving grade four as the highest grade level attainable in the segregated schools. Ross Road School elected its first Board of Trustees at a meeting on November 16, 1970 at the school. The five-member board made up of community representatives from the feeder schools of East and North Preston, Lawrencetown, and Ross Road consisted of: Chairman, Donald Denison; Secretary, Ken Robb; trustee for a three-year term, John Thomas Jr.; trustees for a two-year term, Gerin Ball and Wilfred Simmonds, and trustee for a one-year term, James Slawter. John's three-year term would last for seven years. In June 1972 he was elected chairman of the board, a position he held until March 30, 1977. These trustees worked tirelessly with Ross Road School staff and parents in helping all children who were struggling. At the time, when integrated schools were still in their infancy, it was important to have board members who were aware of the achievement gap that existed between black and white children.

Classes from primary to grade four continued at Partridge River School. Staff worked hard helping the students improve their grades and put in extra time preparing students for Christmas concerts, field trips, and school outings. Over the years Partridge River students were fortunate to have had many good, caring teachers such as Jean Evans, Dr. Marie Hamilton, Delbert Hodges, and Walter Borden, and, later, Georgina Harper, Florence Bauld, Patricia (Dymond) Riley, Kamlish

Georgina Harper's grade four class, Partridge River School, East Preston, 1974. Georgina was a strict teacher and good at motivating difficult students.

invisible shadows

Bhalnaga, Patricia (States) Riley, George Jewell, Sherrolyn Riley, and Nancy Sparks. They also had the support of home economics teachers Betty Wright and Gertrude Tynes and industrial arts teacher Noel Johnston. A few white teachers, Muriel Tupper for one, taught at Partridge River School and took a serious interest in their students. The school was truly blessed with its first principal, H.A.J. Wedderburn, followed by Inez Cromwell, Doris Evans, Gerald Tynes, Douglas Trider, Leo Isaacs, Sandra Best, Carl Purcell, and Gus Sidhu. These teachers, along with trustees Allan Evans, Samson Williams, William Thomas, James Slawter, William Diggs, Aubrey Glasgow, Carleton Evans, John Thomas Jr., John Saunders, and others, kept the doors to Partridge River School open over the years. Following the outcry of several young community parents who wanted to have their children placed in an integrated school environment, the doors of Partridge River School were closed in 1978. Before the doors closed, Connie Glasgow became the first student of Partridge River School to graduate from university, obtaining her bachelor of arts degree in 1972 from Mount Saint Vincent University. A couple of years after the

Partridge River School, East Preston, ca. 1967. It was in this school that community children received their basic education.

Little Black Sambo, 1899. This fictional character depicts some common stereotypes of black people—knotty hair, rolling eyes and thick, red lips.

school closed, it was destroyed by fire. As I watched our school being consumed by flames from my living room window, I thought, "Just as in 1792, Preston is without a school."

In Preston, black children were introduced to racial prejudice at a young age. In the late 1950s, one of our great black leaders, Dr. W. P. Oliver, raised concerns about the derogatory nature of *Little Black Sambo*, a book in the public school curriculum. Written in 1899 for six- and seven-year-old children by Helen Bannerman, *Little Black Sambo* is the story of a black boy and his adventure in the jungle; by outwitting four conceited tigers, Sambo saves his umbrella, purple shoes, and red coat, and he and his parents, Black Jumbo and Black Mumbo, enjoy a fantastic feast of buttered pancakes. The original publication as well as various American versions from the 1920s, 30s and 40s served to reinforce stereotypes of black people as primitive creatures with greedy eating habits. With children of my own in school at the time, I was worried about the harmful effects of the story's racial overtones, and didn't want to see black children being taunted with "Black Sambo" and "Sambo." *Little Black Sambo* was banned from the public schools on the grounds that it was offensive and humiliating to black people.

In the 1950s and 60s, the Department of Education was still placing permissive licensed teachers without bachelors of education in Nova Scotia's black schools. At this time a densely populated school in the Preston area was in need of teachers. The students were well behind in their grades—many children aged twelve and thirteen were only in grade four. The principal of this school, Fitzgerald Jones, was a member of the African United Baptist Association Education Committee. He recommended to the Halifax County school inspector that I teach a grade four class at his school. After I met with the inspector, he told the principal that I didn't have to wait for my licence, I could start teaching the next day.

A wife and mother of two little girls at the time, I wasn't prepared to start right away and was more than willing to wait for approval of my license before taking the position. I was approved quickly and when I went to get my permissible license, the inspector complimented me and told me with a smile that I "could teach in any coloured school in the province of Nova Scotia." This "coloured" clause came as a shock and I asked what would happen if I wanted to teach in a white school. "Oh! No!" he replied, the licenses were for teaching in black schools and he listed the names of several black teachers who had such licenses. He felt pleased that he could present me with such a license. But, Oh! If you could have seen how red his face turned when I told him that I considered the licence an insult to my race, that I refused to accept a licence based on colour and not qualifications. These licenses clearly told me that being black qualified me to teach black children but not white. I took no form of teaching certificate from the Department of Education until the early 1970s, when I received my Teacher's Aide Certificate at Ross Road School, an integrated school where I taught all children. It has never been my style to take cheap grace and quick answers. Those permissible licenses could be used to undermine positive development in the education of black children. Permissive licenses were necessary in the 1920-1940 era, when the segregated system kept the door to basic education open in black communities, but not in 1959.

In 1954 the reference to separate schools and race was removed from the statutes, but it took another fifteen to twenty years to see any real phasing out of segregated schools. In 1962, a survey showed that the average black woman achieved only a grade six education and the average man achieved even less. According to a 1964 survey, there were about ten thousand black Nova Scotians; among them there were only two lawyers, six ordained ministers, two doctors, and about thirty teachers. Following this report, students at Partridge River School were tested. Because so many slow learners were detected, the Department of Education offered a special auxiliary program to Partridge River School. The program was focussed on helping slow learners, particularly in reading, and teachers were offered an increase in salary to administer the program. As the president of Partridge River Home and School Association and as a parent, I, along with a couple of teachers and many other parents, had concerns about this auxiliary program. Once placed into the program, would students be able to get out? Would the student have to wear the mark of "slow learner" or be labelled stupid? What effect would such a program really have on a student already struggling with reading? As it turned out, the program was not particularly successful and students continued to leave Partridge River School unable to read. They remained in auxiliary and general educational classes throughout the rest of their school years. It did nothing to eliminate the extremely high percentage of high school dropouts and the low numbers of university graduates.

In 1970, the students at Partridge River School once again underwent an evaluation through the Department of Education, the purpose of which was to determine how many students were struggling to obtain a basic elementary education. The psychologist reported fifty children at Partridge River School were in need of auxiliary and remedial assistance and approximately all students were at a reading level well below their grade standard. The local community trustees board presented ideas on how to help the students to the Department of Education. They called for a reduction in class size and the hiring of specialized staff. Instead, in 1972, the Department of Education reduced the teaching staff at Partridge River School from eleven to eight teachers, thus creating a class load of forty students per teacher.

Through John's work as a trustee and my involvement with the Home and School Association, we were shocked to learn that so few students were achieving beyond a grade six or seven level and that nearly every student dropped out before completing high school. I began thinking that for far too long this had been black people's custom,

invisible shadows

myself included. When I was growing up, my parents, like most at the time, could not afford to pay for me to get to school and to buy books, yet I was at a loss as to why students in the 1960s were not staying in school when the school provided transportation and textbooks. Was it because the children were not exposed to an environment where academic success was valued and considered necessary? If so, I saw myself as responsible in some way to change this negative pattern.

I began by dealing with the fact that I too was a high school dropout. At the time I was a mother, busy sterilizing baby bottles, changing diapers, doing laundry, and all the other things that caring for my babies entailed. Although motherhood was one of my life's greatest experiences, the urge to return to school began to creep into my mind.

It was a given that the educational system emphasized white values, but I had a deep feeling I could excel and do something to make a difference. The community people were a simple, God-fearing people who expected little and made do with less. They had large families and young people became carbon copies of their parents and grandparents, carrying on the same traditions, customs, and superstitions as their ancestors. Community residents had limited knowledge of the outside world and children only left their backyards to go to school and church. Here I saw children growing up in a community where the rate of unemployment was high, especially among men, where people who did work often took menial, dead-end jobs, and where the children did not see success around them. Children were often not exposed to an integrated environment until they were bussed out of the community to high school. They felt uncomfortable learning to cope within a diverse society and the easiest thing to do was to drop out of school. Segregation had many drawbacks, but for me the biggest was that it spoiled my opportunity to meet outside people who might challenge my thinking and help me broaden the community agenda.

Wanting to be an inspiration to my children and others, I returned to school. Remember, this is the early 1960s, a time when women were expected to remain in their preordained roles of mother and homemaker. In 1962, I registered for night classes at Graham Creighton High School and found myself the only black person in a class of sixteen adults. After being out of school for years, I experienced some difficulties. My brains had become a little rusty and having three children to take care of and holding onto a part-time job gave me very little time for study and homework. French was my weakness and most of my study time was devoted to this subject. Algebra required a little extra time, but I could keep up with the best of them in English, history and other subjects. My most difficult year was my last year at Graham Creighton. I was pregnant. Nevertheless, I had come too close to receiving my high school diploma to quit now. I was ever so glad when I found out another woman in the class was pregnant too. I wasn't the only one there in a maternity suit.

The year after completing high school, I went on to take a one-year, five-day-a-week course at the Nova Scotia Technical College. This course kept my nose in textbooks learning shorthand, typing, bookkeeping, and dictaphone. Upon receiving my diploma, I put my school days aside for a while to spend more time helping my children with their homework as I now had three children in school and three at home. When all my children were in school, I wanted to take some university courses, which in the 1970s cost $150 to $175 per course. Although I was registered at Saint Mary's University and received some university credits, there came a time when I could no longer afford to continue my education there. Yet I didn't let finances extinguish my interest in education. I continued on to take various courses such as: leadership, community development, teacher aide, Red Cross home nursing, Bible studies, pre-school childcare, computers, and writing. Who knows, one day I may return to university and graduate with my grandchildren just to prove to them what my daddy told me, "education is no load to carry and never get the idea that you know too much to learn more."

Since taking the step to return to high school, I have seen great changes in community residents' attitudes towards the necessity of education. Increasingly, young men and women five to ten years my junior returned to school and obtained new skills and training. Today's children begin their education in an integrated environment and there are no fees for high school textbooks, which gives all students the opportunity to complete their high school education. Many still drop out, and when they encounter problems finding employment, they short change themselves by looking for quick-fixes to their educational problems. It would be really great if more of our black children would hang in so they could come out on an equal footing and with pride and dignity prepare themselves to compete in Canadian society.

It was never my custom to handle the problem of racism in the manner I believe that white society expects black people to: retaliation. I refused to fly off the handle and rant and rave about the injustices that I faced. During the years of raising my family, the cruelties of discrimination came thick and fast. There were so many methods used to prevent black children from receiving an education, it was unreal. I started my children in a segregated school knowing that to get ahead in life they must be properly educated, but there they were receiving substandard education in overcrowded, ill-equipped classrooms with scarcely enough desks, blackboards, and chalk and with some teachers possessing limited educations themselves. Despite these conditions, in the 1970s our daughter Wanda went on to Graham Creighton High School, where she was encouraged by John and me to take a full course load. We were surprised to learn that the vice-principal felt she would not be able to handle the full seven courses. Despite this reservation, she carried a full course load throughout high school and went on to complete a bachelor's degree at Dalhousie University.

Dealing with racism also meant teaching my children to deal with it. It was after leaving Mount Denson that I first learnt that mainstream white society deemed black people untrustworthy and unintelligent. There are racial events and feelings I will never forget: the anger of being followed in a store, being rejected while seeking employment, applying and being rejected for a loan at the bank. When my children came along I knew I had to prepare them to deal with the fear of rejection. They were born into a society with strong racist undercurrents that make black people believe it is useless to try to work toward long-term life goals—a belief that robs black children of hope and vision. From an early age, they got the message that it is a white world: from fairy tales with white kings, queens, princesses and princes to white dolls and superheroes. Even in black churches, God is white. It was of utmost importance to me to instil pride, dignity, and self-esteem in my children. I made black rag dolls for my daughters to play with. It may have been a small thing but I felt it helped counteract the effects of the negative racial images that were everywhere.

Hearing about unfortunate things that happened to black people wasn't like experiencing it. Some things can be taught, other things have to be lived to be really understood; such was segregation with me. I modified my parent's method of dealing with racism and came up with a style of my own. I came to understand that to be black you had to live in two worlds, play by two sets of rules, and struggle to maintain your sanity when those two realities collided. I knew it was important to make our children feel comfortable around non-black people. Each summer, the children and I went home to Mount Denson for a week's vacation so they could spend time with the children at the Hantsport Community Centre playground. The interaction my children had with these white children made it easier for them to fit in when they entered integrated schools.

Rev. W. P. Oliver had a philosophy that self-confidence was the first step toward believing that blacks can learn and accomplish as well as others. Maybe it was this philosophy that caused him to look beyond the statistics and see the needs of black school children. He understood that black students needed to be motivated to stay in school. This insight led to his founding of the Education Incentive Fund for black Nova Scotian students in April 1965. Realizing that educators alone could not solve the educational problems facing black people and that the poverty-stricken black communities could not assist their students in obtaining suitable clothing, textbooks, and school supplies, Oliver developed a proposal for ways in which government could assist black students. A fund with a budget of $25,000 in its first year was set up and administrated through the Department of Welfare to assist 350 black students. In 1972, at a time when the door of employment to black Nova Scotians was just starting to open and parents were still struggling and juggling to provide their families with the bare necessities, the fund's annual budget increased to $100,000. Black students in junior high school received from $20 to $30 per year and senior high students received from $90 to $120 per year. Although these funds did not cover the annual cost of a child's education, they were a help to needy students coming from poor families.

The name of the program was changed in 1980-81 to the Education Incentive Program for Black Students. It shifted money from the funds to a $3,000 university scholarship for black students achieving a seventy-five percent average in grade twelve. Starting in 1990-91, the program's total funding was dedicated to post secondary education. The program increased the scholarship to $4,500 for black students who completed grade twelve in the public school system with a seventy-five per cent or better average in their graduating year. Twenty-nine black students met these requirements in 1991-92.

Slowly but increasingly, Preston's residents were beginning to believe that if they wanted to improve the quality of their lives and overcome the effects of discrimination and segregation, they would have to make their political views known. Tired of waiting for political, social, educational, and above all economic improvements, a small number of community residents began exerting political pressure on their white elected politicians. One of the well-known leaders of our community was Allan W. Evans, appointed county councillor in 1931. Black people were living in critical times and were being denied their full rights and privileges of citizenship. Councillor Evans always put into proper perspective the needs and claims of the black people of Preston. He never treated the questions of politics and economics lightly. Although he had strong ties to the Nova Scotia Progressive Conservative Party, he didn't hold any blind devotion to this party and was never just an errand boy at election times. He took part in campaigning for conservative MLAs and MPs, and if they were elected, he tried very hard to have these political incumbents deliver on their promises to his people.

There was never a time in the history of the township of Preston that more progress was made than during the reign of Allan Evans. He let it be known throughout the district that the township of Preston was built on the backs of black people who took seriously their investment in the community. His words were true. It was our black forbears who laboured in these lands under the most oppressive and humiliating conditions, without wages in many cases, to open and clear the road into Preston. Up to this very day, if the truth be told, no part of Preston's history can be recorded without taking into account the contributions and participation of black people. Allan Evans served as both a political and religious leader, holding not only the role of county councillor but also the position of deacon in East Preston United Baptist Church. One of Councillor Evans' first tasks as councillor was to bring about the installation of electrical and telephone services to the Preston communities. He played a strong part in the erection of new schools in East and North Preston and, the Saturday before he passed away, saw the pouring of the foundation of the parsonage in Preston to house the minister serving East and North Preston and Cherry Brook churches.

Preston's council seat was filled by William Thomas in 1961. Thomas's major concern was overcrowded housing. At the time, the Air Force Base in Shearwater was erecting new personnel living quarters. Thomas made arrangements to have sections of the old Air Force barracks brought to Preston for those in need of housing. Each section consisted of four or five rooms at a cost of one hundred and fifty dollars. Some were free to those who hauled them away. Several Preston families benefited from these homes.

During Councillor Arnold Johnson's term of office, beginning in 1964, the need for fire protection was addressed and the Lake Echo Fire Department established. Day care facilities in North and East Preston were also put in place. An old Cole Harbour church building was donated to the community of North Preston to house a medical clinic and childcare facilities. Opened in 1971, the centre added a new wing in November 1986 to allow for more space for its fifty-four children. The new wing also houses a combined gym and music room. The North Preston Day Care Centre and Medical Clinic employs community residents.

A few years later, with the support of the Black United Front, Garnet Brown, MLA, Rev. Donald Skeir, and Arnold Johnson, county councillor, the community of East Preston received a $35,212.00 L.I.P. grant and a $10,000 grant from the Provincial Recreation Department to erect their own day care facility. With continued financial donations from both outside and within the community, the East Preston Day Care Centre opened its doors in 1974 with an enrolment of about thirty children. In 1984, it expanded to provide for more children. The centre is still being subsidized by the provincial government as well as by a number of cash and other donations along with its fund-raising projects.

Wayne Adams was elected in 1979 and was instrumental in having the Sarah Jane Clayton Manor built in 1980. This fifteen-unit senior citizens' home went up on the corner of lower Governor Street and the Number Seven Highway. Wayne also became Minister of Supply and Services in the Liberal government's cabinet and later Minister of Environment. On September 16, 1998, a portrait of Wayne Adams was unveiled and now hangs in Province House.

Up to mid-century, Preston's leadership came mainly from its church. However, as more black immigrants from the United States, Caribbean Islands, and Africa were coming to Canada after mid-century, black Canadians started viewing their world from different eyes. Past experience of racial discrimination made some community residents realize a strong black civic organization was needed to improve black public image, and the black awakening in the sixties and seventies also had its effects on Nova Scotia. New black immigrants such as Frizzell Jones of the African United Baptist Association Education Committee, H.A.J. Wedderburn of the National Association for the Advancement of Coloured People, and Akintunde Adekayode, a native of Sierra Leone who worked for the newly organized Black United Front, were instrumental in the changing shape of Preston's political landscape. Along with Rev. W.P. Oliver from the division of Adult Education, they encouraged black people to get involved in the racial struggle. Their first focus for reform was in the areas of education, employment, and housing. Through reforms, they encouraged greater black pride and awareness.

Although the feminist movement was another powerful social

movement taking hold in Canada past mid-century, there was no such thing as feminist consciousness-raising groups in Preston. The only women's groups in Preston were organized through the church. In my day, women held onto the tradition that both authority in the family and responsibility for its economic support were shouldered by the man; he was head of the household. The woman's role was as homemaker. This was a time when it never occurred to a black man that a woman could be married and have a career too. John definitely thought I was stepping out of line when I wanted to go back to work, and my resistance to tradition didn't make him feel happy. But I had always felt that a woman's life should consist of more than cooking and climbing a stepladder to clean. I obtained satisfaction from being a mother and homemaker, but I also enjoyed working outside the home. It was a great feeling to earn my own salary and not have to depend on John for every cent I spent. To me, working was more about taking control of my independence than a feminist stance; I was never big within the feminist movement because I never felt that sexism was the main factor denying me an equal place in society. I was more conscious that race as opposed to gender or class oppressed me, and the lack of a critical perspective on racism and discriminatory social practices within the feminist movement was far too important for me to ignore.

During my childbearing years, John, like most black men, took pride in being the breadwinner in our home, but I grew tired of being a stay-at-home mother. Plus, having children put a major strain on our household budget. I decided to get a job. Not knowing when another pregnancy may occur, I only accepted part-time employment. My decision came at a good time—in 1959—as the provincial government was looking for Medical Service Insurance (MSI) enumerators. My work as an enumerator for part of Preston took me into a great many homes throughout the community. While going door to door gathering the necessary information and filling out forms, I got to know a lot of people in the community. Even after I finished this job, residents continued to call on me to fill out income tax and pension forms and grant applications. Some still do to this day.

When MSI enumeration finished, I stayed home for a couple of years until I saw an ad for part-time work while reading the daily paper one evening. Pausing for a second, I thought, "My baby, Wendell, is standing alone, ready to take his first step any day now, but just too afraid to do so." I clipped the ad out of the paper with the intention of calling the next day without saying a word about it to John. During my phone call the next day, I was given a time for an interview with Office Overload. That evening I told John about my interview and he didn't sound too happy when he said, "You won't have a problem getting a job." Sure enough, my job offer came on the day of my interview. I joined Office Overload, an agency that placed temporary staff in various offices. I worked in some placements for a day or two and in others for a few weeks or months. My duties varied from clerical, typing, and general office assistance to bookkeeping. It was nice having a second salary coming in again although I missed being home with the children.

Wendell was still walking under the kitchen table without touching his head when my pregnancy with Miles started to show. I quit my job (in those days, women stayed in the house most of the time when their pregnancies became noticeable.) There I was, at home again with three children (Wendy, Wanda, and Wendell) and another one on the way. Yet, I truly enjoyed seeing all the little things I had been missing with my children: Wendy feeding the ducks, Wanda taking her doll for a ride in her doll carriage, and Wendell picking wild flowers for me. When I came home from the hospital with Miles, the children were all excited and really proud they had a baby brother. Wendy and Wanda wanted to hold him on their lap. During this time, I saw the children drawing closer to their father. They would follow me from foot to foot until their father came home from work, then he couldn't move without them being there, especially Wendy and Wendell. Wanda still clung to me.

Miles was a jolly little boy. When he was walking around continually pulling the cupboard doors open and always wanting to go outside with Skippy, our dog, it was time for me to return to work. I went back to work with Office Overload, taking temporary placements again. It seemed like I had just started back when I had to quit again. My next pregnancy was more complicated—everything I ate caused heartburn and if I stayed on my feet for a long period of time, they became swollen. I felt so big and awkward that I only went out of the house for my doctor's appointments. I truly was glad when Cordell was born. What a long nine months! The week I went into the hospital was like a vacation. When I brought Cordell home, my days started earlier and ended later. John took night duty at home. Before I returned to work, John and I took our first vacation alone in ten years of marriage. We took the children home to Mumma in Mount Denson for a week while we went across the border to the United States.

Christmas in Preston, 1965. Kneeling from left to right: Wendy, Wendell, Miles and Wanda. Seated: me holding Tina and John holding Cordell.

invisible shadows

Although it was a wonderful vacation, I missed the children and was glad to get back home. In September, Wendy, Wanda, and Wendell were off to school and I went back to work.

My third placement with Office Overload was at Major Vending, a company whose vending machines were in institutions, offices, and at work sites. There were several offices on the first floor of this building and a huge kitchen on the lower floor where sandwiches and other supplies for the vending machines were prepared. I worked on the first floor in a small office referred to as the "money room." This little office was equipped with a huge floor safe, a money-sorting machine, an adding machine, and other banking necessities. My duties were to operate the machines and help the clerk make up the daily bank deposit, which was picked up by the "Brinks boys." After I had been there for about a month, the banking clerk I was working with took another position with the company and recommended me

Camping in the valley, 1967. This picture was taken in Robert States' 'apple orchard. From left to right: Cordell, Wanda, Wendy, Tina, Miles, Wendell and John. Cordell is sullen because we came to the orchard before stopping at the store for his Cracker Jacks.

for her banking clerk position, which meant I would be working alone in the money room full-time, five days a week. The keys to the office and safe would be turned over to me. There was trouble in our camp again when I told John about the job offer. (At this time he was working as a stationary engineer with the federal government and had employee benefits.) He felt that the job held an element of danger, and that I could become a target for robbery. He also didn't want the children left with a babysitter five days a week. Ever stubborn, I left Office Overload and took the position at Major Vending. Viola, John's cousin, babysat and took excellent care of our children. A couple of years later, I became pregnant again and, not having any maternity benefits, I gave up my job. Tina received a big welcome when she came home from the hospital. Being a girl with three boys between her and her two older sisters, she received a lot of attention. Tina and Cordell were so much like twins that Mumma called them Buffy and Jody.

Working outside the home had many advantages for me. It's true, it meant twice as much work for me—working all day on the job and half the night at home. Nevertheless, it gave me great satisfaction knowing I was a financial contributor in our household. It also gave me new skills and the opportunity to meet people from many walks of life. Working day after day meant learning and putting into practice various office skills and coping with the different personalities around the office. And meeting a diversity of people, young and old, learning, working, and playing together gave my ever growing consciousness of race a new outlook.

It was a good feeling to know that Mumma was pleased with me being a working mother. When she came to visit, we talked about work outside the home. As a working mother herself, Mumma clearly understood my desire to take a paying job. She told me my salary would help John and I move ahead a little faster than would his salary alone. As she stated, "every penny counts when you are just starting out in life." Mumma's visits meant a lot to me. Living in Preston so far from my parents, I couldn't always get to visit them as often as I would have liked. Therefore, it was truly quality time to me whenever we saw

invisible shadows

each other. Whenever I went home, I took Daddy a treat of humbugs and peppermint candy, which he always kept on the little stand at the head of his bed.

As I was getting out of bed on Sunday morning, May 31, 1964, the telephone rang. John took the call and the look on his face told me something terrible had happened. He took me into the bedroom, sat me on our bed, and told me he had some bad news about Daddy. That very minute I knew daddy had died. He had taken a heart attack just before 8:00 a.m., knock-off time at work. When we arrived home to Mount Denson, some family members and friends had already started to gather at our house. The family doctor was still with Mumma. She was sedated. Daddy's death had a tremendous effect on our whole family as well as on his co-workers and friends. Everyone in the community was so kind and thoughtful, bringing us food and helping to ease our pain. I lost a wonderful father and only those who have lost their father know what that is like.

While I was working at Office Overload, John had started to build our house. He had dug the foundation out with a pick-axe and shovel, and laid cement blocks—what he lacked in carpentry skills he made up for in determination. After his eight-hour work day, he spent his evenings sawing, hammering, and singing as he built our home. He didn't know the words to the popular songs of the day so he added his own words and sang away. Some evenings one of his friends, Leo Brooks, Reggie Williams, Rebeau Williams, or Carl Evans, would drop by to give him a hand. Sometimes I helped by holding a piece of wallboard up with a broom until he secured it with a few nails.

We moved into our home before the furnace and plumbing were done and were thankful for more space. I continued to work from job to job. While I was working for Nova Scotia Light and Power, we hired a babysitter who proceeded to steal many of our wedding gifts, a set of dishes, family pictures, and school supplies. She cleaned us out before we discovered it. This put an end to my employment at the Nova Scotia Light and Power until all six of our children were in school. In the winter of 1962, our principal heat came from the wood and coal kitchen range and living room fireplace. We were still using the outhouse, as the only inside plumbing was the cold water tap in the kitchen. With no outside drain pipe for the kitchen sink, the water drained into a ten-gallon pail in the closet under the sink. John was kept busy keeping the big pail empty.

In the spring of 1963, things started to change, and we had an oil heating system installed. Inside plumbing was done in 1964. It was quite costly, which meant we couldn't afford to purchase a couple other smaller items we needed—linoleum for the hall floor, for one. Every time I walked down the hall my patience wore more and more thin, until it was worn right down, just like the pattern on the old linoleum floor. I set to work with some leftover paint I found in the basement. First, I painted the entire floor grey. On day two, I stuffed a soup can with a rag, squeezed the top of the can together enough to hold the rag in place, dipped the rag end in green paint, and dappled it over the floor. On day three, I used the same method with red paint. On day four, I continued with yellow paint. On day five, I went shopping for a can of clear shellac and a new paint brush. On day six,

My beloved home in Preston.

invisible shadows

after putting the children to bed for the night, I started the shellac job. When John told me I might need two coats of shellac, I decided to turn the finishing process over to him. Before coming to bed that night, he had completed the job. In the morning when the children saw the glossy finished floor they were all excited about "the new floor Mummy made." This was just one of the many times we made do with what we had. Our wood and coal range was replaced with an electric range in 1965. As the children curled up in front of the fireplace to watch TV on a cold winter night, it made us feel good knowing that our family could enjoy these home comforts and that we didn't have a mortgage hanging over our head. We were fortunate that John was one of the few people in the community with a permanent job.

As a family, our lives were made up of a network of routines and

Christmas, 1968. Every year, I prepared the traditional candlelight refreshment trays of Christmas cake, cookies, nuts and a punch bowl of Christmas syrup.

rituals—the annual after school barbecue in the backyard, the Easter egg hunt, the search for the perfect Christmas tree, picnicking at the beach, tenting in Grand Pré. In 1969, I struck upon the idea of making a family park out of our plot of woodland on Cooper's Hill. In the fall, we took a saw, pickaxe, axe, shovel, two rakes, and a wheelbarrow to the site and set to work. John cut down the trees and built an outhouse while the children and I raked up around the stumps and carted off the debris. After a rain, while the ground was still wet, we burnt the brush. We were often exhausted after a day's work—our backs ached and our callused hands throbbed—but it was a happy exhaustion. After three years of work, I applied for an L.I.P. grant to hire a few high school students for the summer. Lee Thomas hauled wood out by horse, Derrick Williams raked and cleaned, and Jeffery Williams built picnic tables. In the spring of 1972, John built cement barbecue pits. Wanda and Miles painted the tree stumps, which would be used as seats, and Wendell and Cordell raked and placed garbage cans throughout the park. Wendy, Tina, and I papered the outhouse. During the winter woodwork classes, I made a sign for the park. John hung the "Thomases' Jil-R-Wet Park" sign and from the summer of 1973, the park was used for family outings and group camping. Shortly after John's passing, the sign came down and the picnic tables have since been removed, although the Brownies and Guides continued to use the park for Think Night activities.

Once all the children were in school, I took a teacher's aide position at Ross Road school, which allowed me to leave and return home with our children. This made John happy and he became comfortable with the fact that I was working outside the home. Because of John's benefits and my own salary, our family didn't have to bear the hardships and miseries that some community families did. We didn't have the very best in material advantages or most of the modern conveniences of today, but we always managed to live comfortably.

Housing has undergone many changes in the years since I first moved to Preston. There were always some homes of sound structure in Preston, like Albert Crawley's house which was first located on lower Governor Street across from the old Crawley's Road, then moved across the field to the Number Seven Highway. Where we lived in Preston, the houses were scattered in some places for quite a distance. Most of them were small wooden structures with tar paper siding and most didn't have electricity, plumbing, running water, or a telephone. A stovepipe pointed up out most of the houses to the sky, belching smoke. At night the yellow orange light from a lamp or candle lighted a window. Most houses were not built with new lumber, and only a couple of log cabins were to be seen. Usually, the men collected doors, windows, lumber, and other used material from demolished buildings and recycled it into the family home. These homes only had the bare essentials, and not every floor was covered with linoleum. Some families shivered in the cold as they listened to the wail of the wind slipping through the treetops and whistling through the cracks and crevices in their homes. The rising wind shook loose windowpanes and loose floor boards rattled when someone walked across the floor. But they were homes in every sense of the word, with doors open to all. Regardless of how full a home may be, if someone needed a place to stay, room was found. There were no homeless people in Preston. Everybody in the community was cared for by someone.

Albert Crawley moving his home from lower Governor Street to its present location on Highway 7, ca 1948. Albert is fifth from the left.

It wasn't until late 1960s that the government decided to take a look at living conditions in the black communities throughout Nova Scotia. Here was a man on the moon and yet, the black settlers of Nova Scotia, after having been here for more than two hundred years, were still living in squalor. Following a tour of the Preston area in June 1969, Federal Health Minister John Munro said he was shocked at the deplorable conditions that existed in Preston. At a press conference in Halifax, he announced that some health department personnel were remaining in Halifax to study the situation and needs further. The study clearly pointed out that Preston's situation had been ignored by all levels of government, particularly county officials. The report singled North Preston out as squalor: a forgotten area. The county's Unsightly Premises Inspector had never seen Preston before, nor had the Chief Building Inspector ever made a personal tour. When all these authorities, including a welfare committee, made a tour of Preston, they reported families, some with twenty children, squeezed into two-room shacks with only a wood stove for warmth and with-

Originally Ernest Ewing's house, Kane's house is one of the oldest homesteads in Preston. Ca. 1970.

out a privy or well. Some of the homes were fire traps. The welfare chairman said he saw paper-thin and rusted stove pipes almost touching cardboard walls and reaching through cardboard ceilings. Following the study, the recommendations indicated that public funds were needed to reverse this deplorable situation.

Because banks and insurance companies had red-lined the community, it had been impossible for blacks in Preston to get mortgages. However, after the study, the Nova Scotia Housing Commission instigated a program to assist Preston's low-income families improve their living conditions. The banks and mortgage companies opened a line of credit to people in Preston, thus enabling community residents to improve housing standards. In a short time, the greatest housing boom in the history of Preston took place. Everywhere, it was up with the new and down with the old, and a new sense of pride spread through Preston. This was also a time when many family were beginning to pull themselves up with the assistance of welfare.

Preston residents were for the most part law-abiding citizens. It was certainly not a high crime rate area and the few misdemeanours that took place in the community were dealt with by community members. If something went missing from someone's backyard, barn, or house, residents usually knew who to question and they dealt with it personally. When I came to Preston, it wasn't the custom to lock your doors. Folks dropped by at all hours to borrow a cup of sugar, swap tales, or catch up on a little gossip. One Monday morning during one of my pregnancies, I was setting in a neighbour's kitchen when two white men, one carrying a gun, opened her door and walked into the house. One man asked her for some beer. When she told him she hadn't any, he told her he knew she was a bootlegger and that she had some beer. My neighbour again told them she had no liquor in the house and asked them to go, pointing to me saying, "She is pregnant and you are scaring her to death." Then the other man pointed the gun at her and demanded, "a half-dozen beer, now!" In my state of shock, I stood up and screeched, "Don't shoot her." The one by the door said, "Oh God, she is having a baby. Let's get out-of-here!" I saw from the kitchen window they were driving a red truck so I suggested we call the police. "We don't call the police out here," my neighbour told me, "they won't do anything to a white person who does something to a coloured person in Preston."

The County of Halifax placed black county constables in the Preston area. They made citizens arrests, served court summons, directed traffic during large community gatherings, mediated in domestic and community disputes, collected taxes, and paid the community school teachers. It was the county constable that the community residents put their trust in to maintain law and order in their community. These county constables were in place before I came to Preston and I heard many stories about constables John Thomas, Joe Evans, and Richard Brooks. Constable Richard Brooks was a descendent of William Deer and grew up at the Stag Inn in Preston in the 1870s. Throughout the course of his duties as a constable he maintained respect for his fellow community residents and, as a result, was respected throughout the Preston area. He was the last serving constable in Preston, carrying out his duties until his eightieth year. Constable duties were taken over by the RCMP in the early 1950s.

Preston residents had a hard time trusting the RCMP and hesitated calling in the police to deal with crime. It seemed to them that black offenders were placed under a spotlight for the simplest misdemeanours and that the media coverage was overly negative and unfair. Residents told many stories about how black men were kicked and roughed-up when taken to the police station. Many people felt that the RCMP only came into the community when called in an emergency involving potential loss of life—for example an accident. When called because of fighting, drunkenness, theft, or family disputes, they rarely came. In the case when they did come, it was well after the fight was over or the problem had been taken care of by a community member. Many residents felt the RCMP were actually afraid to enter the Preston communities. This slowly began to change in the mid 1970s when a police car started to pass through the community or park near the community centre waiting to catch someone drinking or carrying liquor. A few years later, police cracked down on community bootleggers and residents began to have more favourable attitudes towards them. In the 1990s, community police programs were set-up with a community police office at the Black Cultural Centre and special black community RCMP constables trained to carry out the duties of community policing.

Whenever fire occurred, community men came to the rescue and fought the fire by bucket-brigade. This was a slow method and sometimes both lives and homes were claimed by fire before the nearest fire trucks arrived on the scene. In March, 1941 two children perished when fire levelled their home in Preston. Councillor Evans received burns about his head as he sought to enter the flaming dwelling in an effort to rescue the two little children.

Because there were still not many vehicles in Preston in the late fifties, people depended on the few that were here to help them during emergencies. John answered many late night and early morning calls to take a neighbour to the hospital or the doctor, or take a midwife to an expectant mother. In January 1959, John and I answered a call to pick up Reuben, Freda Williams, and their little daughter Carla Ann to take them to separate appointments. We dropped Freda at the Grace Maternity Hospital where she would give birth that night to her daughter Paula, we dropped Reuben at the Halifax Via Rail Station for his porter's duties on an overnight run to Montreal, and we took Carla Anne, who had a bad cold, to see the doctor. As I cuddled little Carla Anne in my arms during our ride back home to Preston, little did I know that this would be her last car ride. We took her home to her grandmother Williams' house. On that next bitter cold January morning, fire raced through the Williams' home. Carla Anne, her grandmother, Annie Williams, and two other grandchildren were trapped inside. Carla Anne's two uncles, aunt, and cousin Margaret got out of the burning dwelling. Unfortunately, against the many cries not to go back into the burning house, Margaret went back in to save her grandmother. This wasn't to be and in her attempt, she lost her own life. The nearest fire trucks from Dartmouth arrived on the scene too late. Such tragedies had a devastating effect on the whole community.

With the changing of community leadership during the 1970s

and 80s, the last of our few basic community services such as the post office, the school, small grocery stores, and the opportunity to have District 8 Fire Station located in Preston (the district's central point) were forfeited. Deprived of these services, the community became further isolated. It would have been advantageous to have had the fire station located in this area rather than on the outskirts, because the community, with its many lakes and rivers, had excellent access to water. The majority of residential structures in Preston could have been demolished under provisions of the Fire Protection Legislation. However, the needs of Preston's residents fell on deaf and uncaring ears. Nevertheless, Lake Echo Fire Department, a very fundamental service in our community, opened its doors in 1973, offering services to the communities of North and East Preston, Salmon River, Lake Echo, part of Porter's Lake, and a portion of the Minesville and Crowell Roads to the south of Highway 107. The volunteer firefighters operate all apparatus, rescue equipment, and vehicles during an emergency response. This fire protection service has prevented many tragedies in Preston. Since their beginning they have opened a substation in North Preston. Some of the volunteer firefighters, including my daughter Tina, came from North and East Preston.

Although when I came to Preston in the 1950s unemployment was rampant, my next door neighbour, James Slawter, told me that in the 1930s the Depression hit the black community especially hard. "Times were so hard," he said, "that it was only the mercy of the Lord that kept some of our people living." James Slawter, Benny Evans, and Peter Clayton were the overseeing officers of the poor for East and North Preston, issuing relief according to family size and need. Even after the 1930s, social inequality in the workplace kept black people concentrated in the lowest paying and dirtiest jobs. The majority of black men who were employed in the labour force were employed in unskilled jobs, and black women were domestic workers. Blacks worked the hardest and were paid half as much as whites. They laboured in these conditions because the only alternative was starvation.

Albert Crawley remembered making fifty cents a day before World War One. After the war, he helped lay the first track at the Arm Bridge in Halifax for thirty cents an hour. Other men worked as manual labourers in Halifax and Dartmouth, mixing cement, doing odd carpenter's jobs and farm work. Those who became bricklayers earned about forty cents an hour in 1935-36, and general labourers were paid thirty-five cents an hour. Some of the greatest bricklayers, masons, cement finishers, and plasters you ever wished to meet could be found in Preston. William Carter could lay stone with the best of them. He built many stone walls in Dartmouth and along the Eastern Shore and stoned many of the wells in Preston, including my own. Carpenters like James Colley worked with the Brookfield Construction Company to build the Army Barracks at Colley's Hill in 1942. James' father was boss carpenter for this company. His father's salary was $1.10 per hour for a ten-hour day. One of the feats that James remembers accomplishing was drilling a 410-foot well in a six-inch hole for the army's water supply. It took one month to drill the hole. The well was still being used in the 1980s when the last family moved off the old army property. The army had a cannon sited on the plot of land where Clara Gough now lives. When the barracks were torn down, the

Preston men are renowned for their masonry. Ca. 1960.

guardhouse and cookhouse were remodelled into family dwellings and the cannon was moved to the corner of Portland Street and Commercial Street (now Alderney Drive) in Dartmouth. James' brother Charles, the church handyman, was a carpenter as well and made wood carvings and coffins for sale.

Many important public buildings throughout the Halifax and Dartmouth area were built on the hard labour of Preston masons, cement finishers, and carpenters. They were responsible for constructing the Halifax Shopping Centre, the V.G. Hospital, and the Grace Maternity. Harris Brown was one of the cement workers on the construction of the V. G. Hospital and Arthur Smith of North Preston, John Williams and Frank Kane of East Preston along with many others built Scotia Square in downtown Halifax.

Seasonal work lasted from April to November or early December, making for a high unemployment rate the rest of the year. During the few weeks before these men could receive their unemployment insurance benefits, it was not uncommon to see a man dragging a tree out of the woods into his backyard. Men sawed split firewood and bundled it by the hundred to be sold for a dollar a bundle. They cut and sold Christmas trees and sold them at the Halifax City Market and door to door throughout Halifax and Dartmouth. The Christmas tree business brought in good money and men in the Preston area depended on this seasonal income to help support their families. This tradition was maintained until the 1970s when it was slowly squeezed out of existence as service clubs such as the Kiwanis, Kinsmen, and Lions set up Christmas tree stands and artificial trees became more popular.

During the winter, some men worked in the woods as loggers. Their day's work began around 7:00 a.m. The men carried their lunch, mainly bread and beans, with them, and enjoyed a cup of tea steeped in a tin can with a wire handle while sitting on a log in the woods. Sometimes they had to drive the logs down the river by standing on them—dangerous work that required extreme care so they didn't fall between the logs and get crushed or killed. The logs from this well-timbered land were taken to the lumbering mills and used for home heating and in products sold at the city market.

Hunting and fishing in these wood lots provided another source of food for struggling families. Deer, bear, porcupine, wild duck, and partridge were plentiful. The men went hunting during the late fall and if luck was with them, they returned home with a deer, a moose, or a bear. This wild meat was shared with family and friends. Fishing brought food and a small income into the family. Oftentimes I watched the men rowing up the lake in boats they had built to catch fish for their family use, to share with neighbours, and to sell.

Men planted and cared for the gardens, did all the maintenance and repair work around their homes, chopped firewood, and cared for the animals. Some men in the community raised pigs, feeding them with swill collected from the restaurants around town. Unfortunately, swill had the terrible disadvantage of attracting rats. There were so many rats scampering in and out of the barns that the barnyard cats were kept busy chasing them down. In late fall, the men would sell pigs and slaughter one for their own use. Once the pig was cut into roasts, hams, bacon, and other cuts, a couple of roasts would be given away to a widow or community elder. For many years community pig growers carried out a good business. Preston pig growers such as John Clayton, Cecil Taylor, Harold Glasgow, William Slawter, John Thomas, Keith and John Williams raised pigs to sell, many which were sold to the Halifax Abattoir. Changes in county bylaws have caused community pig raising to dwindle, leaving Gordon Thomas among the few pig growers in present-day Preston.

Many bootlegging houses could be found throughout the community. Although Preston residents maintained their subsistence through farming, logging, manual labour, and domestic work, many depended on the small compensation they garnered from bootlegging. Having large families to take care of made this extra income necessary. However, bootlegging came with certain drawbacks. Sometimes when people gathered in these houses and got a little too much liquor in them an argument or fight would break out among the men. These men would fight each other one day and greet each other the next as if nothing had happened.

Women and children participated in the economic well-being of their family through the informal economy. In spring the children picked may flowers for their mothers, who put them in small bunches and tied them with string. Children also helped their mothers pick wild berries in season and put them into quart boxes. Blueberries were the most plentiful. In the spring and summer the women arranged the various kinds of ferns, mosses, wild berries, and flowers into baskets and bouquets to sell from door to door in Halifax or in the city market. This produce was packed in the wagon along with the brooms, baskets, bundles of kindling, flower boxes, bean poles, wooden tubs, clothes props, and other items that they sold. The most profitable time of the year for the women, however, was during Christmas. When the men cut down Christmas trees, they also cut pine, fir, and spruce boughs for the women to make into wreaths. The women and children gathered the red berries and pine cones for decorating the wreaths. The men also brought home peat moss, which the women sprayed with gold or silver and decorated with red berries for wall decorations. The first time my eye fell on a display of Preston women's wreaths, decorated garland, and red berry bunches at the city market, something inside of me lit up. To see the women sitting around the tables in this cold market building, laughing, talking, and putting together more wreaths awakened within me the deeper meaning of Christmas. Here the hard-working women were putting their talents to use in the creation of such unique and splendid Christmas decorations. The joy and happiness they shared together as they worked made me want to sing with new meaning the old-time Christmas carol, "Joy to the World."

It was a long trip from Preston to the market. There was no public transportation in Preston so at four or five o'clock in the morning the ox and horse teams started their day's journey down the Preston Highway to the Dartmouth Ferry Terminus to catch the early morning ferry across to the market. These long open wagon trips to and from the market in bitter cold weather left many of these black vendors plagued with rheumatism. "Red hot" bricks or stones wrapped in an old woollen blanket or coat were placed at the travellers' feet for warmth. Sometimes the travellers got off the wagon and walked for a short distance to warm their bodies up a bit. These market trips were all-day affairs; the vendors arrived home in Preston at seven or eight o'clock at night, cold and hungry, sometimes with frost-bitten ears, fingers, or toes.

As well as selling goods at the marketplace in Halifax, women helped with the economies of their families through sharing. Whether a cup of sugar, some flour, a few potatoes, a loan of a tub or washboard, a bit of Vicks Vaporub, or a needle, it gave the women peace of mind to know that whenever they were in the need of something, they could borrow it from their neighbours. Young black people often make a big deal about recycling, but little do many of them know that the black race could be called the inventors of recycling, going back to the days of slavery. Slaves working in their white master's house took table scraps and leftovers back to their cabins and recycled them into a family meal. When a roast of beef was served at the master's house, the black cook took the beef bone and recycled it into a pot of beef stew for her family. Certain parts of a cow or ox—like the head or hocks—were routinely tossed aside as waste, but the black man slaughtering the animal would salvage these parts and give them to the women to make head cheese or boiled hocks. The women would recycle clothing given to them into other clothes or quilts and other household linens. The recycling method was handed down from generation to generation in the black community; black people didn't call it recycling, rather "waste not, want not." This tradition hadn't completely dwindled when I came to Preston. Some women in the community had access to different goods on a regular basis which they could share with others. For example, if their husband was collecting discarded goods from a grocery store, the owner might put aside dented canned food, split bags of sugar or flour to be collected. The women would take these items to share with others. If a woman's husband worked at a construction site where he had access to used lumber, he would share it with the extended family, often at the suggestion of his wife. Some women's husbands hauled discarded items from wealthier homes in Halifax and Dartmouth. During fall house-cleaning time, they would collect some good clean carpet ends to share with others. My kitchen never had a homey feeling without a mat on the floor. Some of my friends' husbands would collect these good carpet ends and offer one to me. I would shampoo it, take the old one off my floor, put the clean, fresh one down and enjoy the coziness it lent to my kitchen.

Some of the women's husbands got to know the butcher very well and if he didn't have any day-old bones, he would sometimes cut up some meat and make up a box of fresh meaty soup bones, which were also shared with neighbours. The bones were put in a pot, and cooked up until the meat fell off. Vegetables were added to the meat to make a pot of beef soup and the bones were removed and given to the dog. Then, there was a dog in just about every backyard.

If a woman was a domestic worker, she was sometimes given old clothes by her employer. If she got a box of rags or old clothes, she shared them with her women friends, who cut these rags into quilt patches and made quilts for our beds. Since children were often under the weather with communicable children's diseases, common colds, cuts and scratches, it was necessary to have a good supply of first-aid items on hand. John and I had a line of credit with a travelling pharmacy. Each month when the station wagon pulled into my yard loaded with all its supplies and remedies, I paid my five dollars monthly payment and got the items I needed. Sometimes, my monthly supplies of aspirins, cough syrup, salve, Minard's liniment, bandages, teething pain gel, Vicks Vaporub, and peroxide exceeded the five-dollar payment. Oftentimes these supplies were shared with families who didn't have what they needed at the time. If a family had no goods to share, they would still receive goods from others in the community. In return, they allowed their children to run errands or to babysit. Because the sharing system was in place, there was no sense of urgency in paying back favours, nor were favours counted up. People were just too glad to be able to pass along what they could or to receive what they needed for their families. Indeed, many women who did not work outside their homes took care of the working women's children. Children born out-of-wedlock were never abandoned by family. If these children could not be cared for by their natural parent, they were taken in by other women within the family. When there were no day-care facilities, being cared for in a home environment gave the children a sense of family as much as it helped with the family's costs.

Community elders shared the workload with the younger people of the community. Elderly women, be they a grandmother or an aunt, helped with caring for the children and taught the younger generations marketable skills like cooking, quilting, and hooking mats. They made up poultices for fingers, cups of home-made root beer, and stories about how to survive in a community where unemployment, poverty, and neglect were commonplace. The children, in turn, would do chores and run errands for the elders. The elderly men worked right along with the young men, cutting and sawing wood, feeding the animals, carrying water and helping with repairs around the house. Elders were very much an essential part of the extended family unit.

Midwives had a special responsibility in the community. They asked no fee for their service and if someone gave them a dollar that was big pay. Midwives delivered the babies; doctors were only called in when the midwife was confronted with a problem during labour or delivery. The moment the midwife arrived, she started making preparation for the delivery by stirring up a hot fire, closing the oven door to ensure the oven heated up, putting plenty of water on the wood stove to boil, and gathering up clean woollen blankets. They never refused a case, even though many calls came in the deep of the night with bitter cold temperatures and snow-blocked roads.

There were several midwives in Preston: Cecilia Brown, Margaret Crawley, and Jane Slawter. They were called at any hour in all kinds of weather to wait on an expectant mother. I was one of those mothers during a bitter winter blizzard on January 20, 1958. Snow had fallen the day before into high drifts along the Preston highway. When the storm eased somewhat, James Slawter, the District Road Foreman, dispatched the snowplow along this highway in an attempt to keep it passable. It continued to snow and the plow had to remain on the highway and could not open any secondary roads in the area. Unfortunately, our home was on one of these secondary roads (Brian Street) just over a hill from the highway. When we awoke on the morning of January 20, 1958, it was still snowing. Our road was impassable, so John stayed home from work. Luckily for me. We were expecting a baby, but certainly not in January, yet I was beginning to feel pain and the baby moving a lot. When I told John, he told me to lie down and he immediately went outside, shovelled his way to the car, and started it. He left the car running while he came into the house to check on me. The pains were coming about every hour and they appeared to be getting more severe. It was obvious John was nervous as he told me he was going for help. Shovelling and driving the car through as much snow as he could to reach the highway, he was on his way to pick-up midwife Margaret Crawley (his grand-mother), known to many as Mum Crawley. She too lived on a sec-ondary road and had to walk a considerable distance to the highway in knee-high snow.

Every minute I waited for John's return seemed like an hour. I became terrified, thinking, "Here I am, pregnant, suffering false labour pains, unable to get to the hospital and too young to die." Finally, I heard voices in the kitchen and Grandma Crawley peeped her head around my bedroom door and said "Thank God we made it, dear. Have you been timing your pains? I'll be in as soon as I take off these wet clothes and warm up a bit." She sang as she prepared her-self. When she entered my bedroom I became very, very nervous and she knew it. She told me although it is not my due time, these were real labour pains and the baby was on its way. Before I could panic, she gently said, "All we have to do is put our faith in Jesus and every-thing will be all right." As she prepared me for delivery she was singing, "Never alone, no never alone, He promised never to leave us, never to leave us alone." This was the most peaceful anaesthetic I had ever had. It brought comfort and assurance that everything was going to be all right. However, the real joy hit home when she laid our lit-tle premature daughter in my arms. Then she went into her black satchel, took out some dried leaves, and made me a warm cup of mint tea. A flannelette waistband was put on me to support my back. A flannelette waistband was also put on the baby, whom we named Wanda. Each day for about a week Grandma Crawley came to bathe and dress Wanda and check on me. She made me a warm cup of mint tea every day. If I had any pain or discomfort she gave me an aspirin. I stayed in bed until the ninth day, believed to be the "turning point" day. Grandma Crawley certainly took the best care of Wanda and me.

Grandma Crawley told me how she delivered a baby girl so small she could hold her in the palm of her hand. The baby was struggling for breath when she was born and Grandma blew air into the baby's collapsed lungs to get her breathing. She also told of how she opened the oven door, held the baby in front of the heat, massaged her back, moistened the baby's body with warm olive oil, wrapped her in a heated woollen blanket and placed her in a basket on the oven door. With loving care this little breast-fed baby girl gained weight and was doing great in a matter of a few weeks. Grandma (Margaret) Crawley was born in 1893 to Mary Elizabeth Dixon and John Alfred Carvery and married Edward Crawley. When Margaret came to the community of Preston, she was no stranger to caring for the sick. She was a cook at Halifax Infectious Diseases Hospital and often told me how she harnessed the family horse, hitched it to the wagon, and rode

Grandma
Crawley and Mr.
Bundy, ready for
church, 1958.

from Africville into Halifax to help care for the injured patients during the Halifax Explosion. She put her maternity work skills into practice while working with Dr. Ralph Malcolm, thus obtaining her midwife certificate. Grandma Crawley died in 1980.

Preston residents often found comfort for their aches and pains in traditional home remedies. No doctor lived in the isolated community of Preston and the lack of transportation made visiting the nearest doctor in the town of Dartmouth difficult. Money for doctor's fees and prescription medicine was scarce. Practically every woman in the neighbourhood had a keen knowledge of herbs and how to prepare them in home-made preventative medicine and treatments. However, midwives and older women in the community would be called upon for treatment advice whenever a child took sick. Some herbs—like tansy and the big green mint leaves to relieve stomach pain—were gathered in the late summer and early fall to be dried and stored for the winter. Tansy leaves were also used for menstrual cramps or in a warm foot and leg bath to soothe arthritic aches. There were plenty of tansy leaves growing in our back yard. In the early evening, John and I took the children for a walk or jog out the lower road. If we returned home with tired feet, John gathered some tansy leaves from the backyard and I put them in the foot tub with hot water and a teaspoon of salt. When the water cooled to warm, we soaked our aching feet for fifteen to twenty minutes. Our feet felt so good coming out of that tansy leaves bath that sometimes we danced around the kitchen floor.

In the spring and fall adults and older children would take a tonic known as "bitter tea" to purify and cleanse their blood. This tonic was made from various barks such as the cherry tree bark, poplar bark, alder bark, spruce bark and burdock root. These barks, along with other ingredients, were steeped in a huge pot with a little molasses to sweeten it some. Bitter tea was an excellent name for this tonic—it was so extremely bitter that the first time I took a mouthful, it gave me the feeling my hair was loosening on my head. Adults took a quarter of a cup of this tonic every morning in April and October. The older children were given one or two teaspoons a day. Other home remedies were used back then: couple of live worms tied in a band around the stomach was a sure cure for internal worms; for headache, we tied sliced potatoes around the forehead with a bandanna; onion, vinegar, and molasses were all used to cure coughs; steeped beach leaves were used for asthma; melted goose grease with a little black pepper in it was rubbed on a child's chest for a cold; and a bread poultice was used to draw out a splinter.

Preston's residents made do with what they had when they could, but Preston was not without its entrepreneurs. One of the earliest was William Deer, the Stag Inn owner I used to hear stories about when I first came to live in Preston. Another entrepreneur who I knew personally was Florence Diggs. She kept a small grocery store for forty-three years from 1938 to 1981. During a period of that time she also ran a post office. There wasn't any sign outside Diggs' store and post office but everyone in the community and along the Eastern Shore knew where it was. This was the place where people picked up a bottle of milk, a loaf of bread, and the mail. Whenever someone entered the store, they were greeted with a smile from Mrs. Diggs, her daughter Mildred, or her granddaughter Patsy. Whenever I stopped in to pick up my mail or make a purchase, Mrs Diggs always asked me to join her for a cup of tea. If I was rushed for time, she would give me a cold pop. I often wondered how such a kind-hearted woman like Mrs. Diggs could make a profit. Over the years, Mrs. Diggs' store suffered because of increased competition in Lake Echo and Dartmouth. When her health began to fail and she lost her vision, the doors of her store had to close.

For residents of upper and lower Governor Street, Wilhelmina Riley's little store was more convenient. Over the years, there were other small grocery stores in Preston. Ernest Glasgow's store carried a wider variety of goods and he made home deliveries. Ernest, like Florence Diggs and Wilhelmina Riley, allowed his customers to purchase their needs on "tick" if need be. When the doors of these little stores closed, their owners were left holding the unpaid bills of some of their customers. Unfortunately, there aren't any little grocery outlets in Preston today. The last one, "On Your Way," which was located at the corner of the Number Seven Highway and Upper Partridge

River Drive and run by Jacqueline Thomas, remained open for only a couple years. It shut down in August 1999.

Edith Clayton was another of Preston's entrepreneurs. A sixth generation maple basket weaver, Edith was only eight years old when her mother (Selena Drummond) taught her how to make baskets from maple wood. In 1979, Edith added a shop onto her home from which she sold sewing, fishing, and shopping baskets, the beautiful horn of plenty baskets as well as baby and doll baskets. Edith loved to pass her basket weaving skills onto others. One of my most treasured possessions is the little maple basket she taught me how to make. Her daughter Clara Gough still carries on the maple basket weaving craft at upper Governor Street.

In the 1980s and 90s, government zeroed in on small focus groups in the Preston area. These groups received government funding in the form of initiative grants to help black people in the community set-up small businesses. Although many members from the focus groups opened small businesses, many of them remained in existence for only a very short time. Today, several little start-up construction and landscaping companies still come and go. These little companies create short-term employment for a few community men. While it is true that government created employment equity and black business initiative programs to support the development of business and job opportunities for black Nova Scotians, it appears that when government grants cease these businesses fold. The Enviro-Depot, operated by Marvin Riley and located at the corner of upper Governor Street and Number Seven Highway, is one of the very few small businesses in Preston today.

Some businesses in Preston today—Diggs Sanitation, Crawley's Stone and Construction, and Paula's Place, for example—never received government grants. Paula's Place, owned and operated by Paula Williams and her business partner, Dennis Brown, began in Paula's parents' home on the Number Seven Highway in Preston. Her starting capital of $1,300 came from money borrowed from her father and from a former employer. She purchased a sewing machine and began making, altering, and repairing clothes. A couple of years later, Paula was given the opportunity to take over a sewing business from a woman living in the King Edward Towers on Main and Dunbrack Street. Paula received a small grant from Small Business Development and she and her new partner Dennis pooled their income tax refunds together to take over the business at the King Edward Towers in Fairview. Later they moved to Rockingham Ridge Plaza, where they remain today. With a loan from the Royal Bank, they were able to expand the business to offer a drop-off service for clothes and footwear repairs, dry-cleaning, key cutting, and skate and knife sharpening. At the present time they are expanding their home shop in Preston.

Until recently, transportation influenced a person's ability to get and hold a job. When the Zinck's company established an Eastern Shore bus route in the 1950s, people living within walking distance to the Number Seven Highway could be in Halifax by 11:00 a.m. and return by 6:00 p.m. Tuesday to Saturday. In the 1970s the Black United Front of Nova Scotia put a trial-run bus service in the community for a few months. Public transportation remained a problem in Preston until 1994 when the Beaverbank transit brought some daily bus service to the community. A few years later this service was taken over by Metro Transit. The Halifax Regional Municipality now sponsors this community transit service with five daily runs from Tacoma Drive, Dartmouth to Preston and the Eastern Shore to Grand Desert.

In 1986, the federal government passed the Employment Equity Act as a means of improving the situation for individuals—women, aboriginal people, people with disabilities and visible minorities—adversely affected by certain systems and employment practices. (According to the Employment Equity Act, visible minorities are persons who are non-white in colour or non-Caucasian in race.) The act helped to change the employment situation somewhat for black people. However, we have a ways to go to catch up to our non-black counterparts, who continuously secure better jobs and better salaries, despite having the same qualifications.

Over the past fifteen years, the Employment Equity Act has removed the barriers and addressed the inequalities in the employment situation for many non-black women. These women fit into the workforce like a missing piece from a puzzle. However, black people are often stigmatized by employment equity programs because they tend to be looked at by their co-workers as unqualified. Some traditional stereotyping still looms over the black workers' heads, and they hold subordinate positions while the more dominant and superior positions are held by white people. When I look at the token and special employment equity programs set aside for black people, I get the feeling we are not considered equal to all other races of people. Therefore, I consider these programs a hindrance more than a help. Why, in the year 2001, is it necessary to have such programs in place? How much longer do we have to wait to go through the same channel, the same door, the same process to get the same things as everyone else? I wonder, how much farther along our journey of life do we black people need to travel to reach real freedom and equality in employment and in human rights in general? Black people try to fit into white culture to be accepted by the workforce and their working peers, but to do so they are forced to disguise themselves and take on the mannerisms, speech, and actions of their white work community during work hours. Informal relations with co-workers after hours are equally difficult— either white people don't want to be seen socializing with black people or Blacks are afraid of being accused of trying to be white. Sometimes these black workers do begin to feel superior to other black people and help to degrade their own race, separating themselves when they can from their people to make themselves look more intelligent. When they are back in the community, they might drop this attitude and just blend in or they might try to convince their friends that they are doing things wrong and that they should change to be more like whites. This in turn brings criticism from the black community. Employment equity has become an excuse for society at large to not open its doors to equality. Where they can point to one or two token workers of other races in their workplace, they give little or no thought to the countless thousands that have been locked out of this process.

The same is true for education. In high school, black students are often put into general programs, which don't prepare them for university and ensure their entry into lower paying jobs. Those who could make it to university often cannot afford university tuition and are forced to enter special programs set up for Blacks. When they obtain certificates through these programs, which are considered to be inferior, their chances to progress in life are again set within limits.

Today, people in Preston work as social workers, nurses, lawyers, policemen, firefighters, hospital workers, federal civil service workers, bus drivers, bank tellers, store clerks, and in non-governmental organizations. New jobs have been created due to better education and employment practices. However, the number of people working in professional capacities is still incredibly small.

Sometimes when life becomes overflowing with joy and happiness sorrow creeps in. One evening while John and I were sitting outside listening to a chorus of frogs in the swamp next to our house, John told me about a medical problem he was having. Right then and there I told him I would be making a doctor's appointment for him the next day. Not being one to go to a doctor, he felt it wasn't necessary. Nevertheless, the appointment was made and within a couple of days his many visits to the doctor began. The result was the discovery of a tumour, which had to be removed. He took sick leave from work. The operation was performed in November, 1978. The tumour was not cancerous and within a few months he returned to work. Keeping all of his follow-up appointments and being told he was healthy, John was fine for the next couple of years. Then he started to have some pain, which he immediately reported to his doctor. Blood tests, x-rays, and a biopsy followed. We were definitely not prepared for the devastating diagnosis of cancer. It struck like a hammer.

I spent days in shocked silence, praying that the doctors had made a mistake in their diagnosis. The day he underwent major surgery, my sixth sense told me something was wrong and somehow the world seemed unnaturally still. A short while after his surgery, we were told his cancer was terminal. I found myself caught up in a whirlwind of emotions as I called upon God for help during this painful time in my life. I spent day after day dreading the inevitable while trying to maintain a normal household. My heart was heavy with pain as I drove John back and forth to his many outpatient appointments and sat helplessly by as he became nauseated and dehydrated following chemotherapy treatments. As I sat by his bedside during his many stays in hospital, months turned into a year and the attending doctors suggested putting John into a nursing home to make things easier for me. Of course, neither of us wanted such a thing, nor did our children. He remained in his own home with us until the end.

Every evening I bathed his swollen feet in warm water and dried tansy leaves. This was so soothing to him that he often told me he felt healing in the touch of my hands. After helping him into bed, he would request a gospel song: "All The Way My Saviour Leads Me," "My Saviour First of All," "Every Time I Feel the Spirit," and his favourite, "Whiter than Snow, yes, whiter than snow, Now wash me, and I shall be whiter than snow." He would sing or hum along with me as we shared those precious moments of singing and praying together, not knowing from one night to the next when the final curtain would come down. The children and I did everything in our power to make John's last days on earth as comfortable as possible. On the morning of October 3, 1982, he asked me to take him to the hospital by ambulance and requested that all the children meet around his hospital bed while the hospital chaplain said a prayer over him and his family. When he kissed me good-bye, I experienced an incredible peaceful sensation and knew John was in God's loving care. A few hours later, he passed away. The children were emotionally shattered and in need of my help. I asked God to give me the faith and courage to keep myself together. Mumma, along with family and friends, was a source of strength to me and the children and my faith in God guided me through.

In 1975, John and I had started tucking away a few dollars to take a trip to Africa. Unfortunately, John didn't live long enough to go with me. I did go to Africa, however, on an "Out of Africa" tour with tour host Reverend Eustace Meade, pastor of the First Baptist Church of Toronto. This was a unique experience that gave me a great opportunity to meet local African people and see them at work and play in places where the tourist normally never goes. We also saw missionary work being carried out in rural areas and were treated to an impressive display of Kenyan traditional dancing.

On July 21, 1984, I found myself in Dakar, Africa caught up in a

invisible shadows

cattle jam. The cattle were crossing the road on their way to a Buy and Sell Stock Fair. As the cattle completed their crossing, we continued on our way. The dusty tree-lined road was intriguing as we discovered the simple beauties of nature. The blazing hot sun peeked over the horizon and around every bend we saw a variety of huge trees and rare animals and birds. Half- naked children scampered around huts along the roadside. I was excited to be in the Africa I had heard of and everywhere I looked I saw black people. I remember feeling that my roots were my destiny and quickly realized I had to make every moment of this tour count. After reaching the hotel, I wasted no time in taking a walk around. This was the beginning of my experience. Sunday we attended an inspirational church service and took a tour of a few settlements. During our stay in Dakar we toured several villages and settlements, the Kerel silver and gold markets and art museums. I certainly enjoyed a beautiful African banquet and dance.

It was when our tour guide, Jobe, took us to the island called "Anse St. Bernard" that I got a butterfly stomach. Anse St. Bernard is the westernmost point of Africa, known as the gateway to Europe and America. This island was the centre of the slave trade because of its location. Africans were brought to this island where they were traded or purchased. Men had to be in good condition and could be traded for a little rum or purchased for next to nothing. Children were traded for mirrors, nail polish and lipstick. Young females were the most expensive.

From 1450 to the 1800s, it is estimated that more than fourteen million Africans (this doesn't include the countless millions who died in passage and upon arrival to the Americas) were shipped from Africa to various countries. The slave trade began around the mid-fifteenth century when the Portuguese were trying to discover a sea route to India. During their voyages they made stops at various points along the West African coast for fruit and fresh water. When they reached the peninsula of Sierra Leone, they began their trade in goods such as cheap ornaments and pieces of cloth manufactured in Europe in exchange for ivory and gold.

It didn't take long for Africans to become the chief commodity in the trade business. The Portuguese sold these people into slavery in Portugal, then later in Spain. When the Spanish began to hold territories in the Caribbean, they used the Carib Indians as slaves, but they treated them so poorly that few survived. The Spanish then imported African slaves from Spain, but found they needed even more slaves. In 1505, the first shipload of African slaves from the Guinea Coast arrived directly at the Spanish settlements and from 1515 onward, they were brought regularly by the shipload directly from Africa to the Americas. In 1562, Captain Jon Hawkins was the first Englishman to bring a cargo of Africans to the Caribbean. He sold them into slavery at a profit in the Spanish settlements. Many Europeans made hit and run raids, burning villages and capturing Africans themselves to sell in the Americas. They also encouraged tribal warfare so that they could buy the prisoners of war from the victorious tribe. Along the West African Coast, the European traders built more slave-trading houses, such as that on Goree Island. Situated along many of the islands on the coast, these houses became known as factories.

Taken from their homelands in chains, the Africans began the hazardous voyage from the Guinea coast of Africa to the West Indies and Americas. This terrible voyage between Africa and the Americas was called the "middle passage," because the slave ships went to the Americas before returning to Europe. Africans were packed aboard these ships and kept below deck for days on end. Conditions were appalling with inadequate toilet facilities, no place to wash and no ventilation. Diseases often broke out and many Africans died. Others gave up hope, and jumped overboard to drown. Man-eating sharks always trailed these ships, no doubt with their mouths open to devour the sick and dead bodies being tossed overboard. The surviving Africans became cheap labour in America or were sold directly into slavery.

There are horrifying stories about these slave ship voyages. One story was about the slave ship Zonq which had approximately four hundred African slaves aboard. During the voyage from Africa to America many became sick and died. The ship's captain felt that this loss could hurt him financially, but the Zonq had an insurance policy that would pay handsomely if any part of the cargo had to be thrown overboard to save

invisible shadows

the rest. The captain reported that the ship was short of water and that, in order to reach port, he had to throw the remainder of the slaves overboard. After he was tried and acquitted for murder, he collected enough money from the insurance company to have made the voyage financially successful. It was through this most devastating trade in human slaves that a great many Blacks arrived in the thirteen colonies of Britain, one day to be known as part of the United States. In 1619, a shipload of twenty Africans arrived at Jamestown, Virginia to be traded for food by the captain of a Dutch ship. When the first Africans were brought to the United States, they were sold as indentured servants, gaining their freedom after working for a master for not less than twenty-one years. However, by 1663 both Maryland and Virginia had laws stating that all Negroes or other slaves should be sold to work for life.

Many Africans were sold into slavery on plantations further south. They worked as field hands, trades people and household servants. They were treated inhumanely—beaten, whipped, or worse. The women were raped by their masters. This exploitation of black women on the slave plantation contributed to the rise of a new breed of people and created separation among the black families. By 1860, there were about a half million persons of mixed descent. In the total slave population of about four million, one out of eight was a mulatto. Because the mulattoes were the sons and daughters of the master, they were often treated better than the other black slaves. They became house servants and chauffeurs, escaping from the gruelling farm labour work and the lash of the whip. Thus to the list of atrocities performed by the white slave masters can be added cultural and class prejudice among slaves and their descendants.

From Anse St. Bernard, Jobe took us on the ferry from Dakar across to Goree Island, which is about nine hundred metres long and two hundred metres wide to visit the Goree Island museum, post office, and slave house. The people on this ferry were tourists and Africans going from Goree Island to work in Dakar. Here we visited the place where Africans were kept before being sold into slavery. The slave house is where approximately twenty million Africans were kept shackled in chains. They were fattened like cattle, auctioned off and shipped to the Americas and the Caribbean to work on plantations. I got the worse feeling I ever had when Jobe showed us the slave house. Here, men, women and children were divided and kept in separate sections. Always in chains, they were allowed to leave their hut once a day, to use the toilet. Whenever a slave disobeyed a master, they were tossed into a hole cut into the concrete floor of the slave house and put in chains until their master felt ready to free them.

The young female slaves were kept in a special compartment where they were chained and never allowed out. They had a hole in the floor to use as a toilet. Slave masters went into the young female's compartment and raped them whenever they wished. Tears came to my eyes as I stood in this slave house in the smouldering heat, hearing such a story.

Apparently, only the best African slaves were taken to be sold. Sorrow and confusion stirred within me when told that in 1779, a disease broke out in the slave house and those who were sick were tossed into the ocean to drown. Jobe told us how families were separated. These Africans were led, in chains, through a doorway to waiting boats to begin their voyage of no return. They left the shores of Africa without names, just registration numbers. At their point of destination, they adopted their master's name, and so there was no hope of them finding each other again.

Jobe then took us through an extremely narrow concrete passage to a wharf. This was the passage that Africans, bound in chains, were dragged through to be carried away on a ship to Anse St. Bernard and sold into slavery. The slave ship was thirty metres long and eight metres wide and it carried 350-400 slaves at a time. This slave house on Goree Island was built by the Dutch and is just a short ferry ride from Dakar, the capital of Senegal. Senegal is one of the world's poorest countries, with a sixty-five per cent illiteracy rate. As I stood on this wharf and gazed at the dark sand on the shores of Goree Island, I could not help but question the extraordinary circumstances which took my black ancestors far from this African village to the shores of Nova Scotia, Canada.

There on the wharf, I stopped hearing what Jobe was saying. Looking around me at all the white people present, a queer hatred fell

invisible shadows

over me. The next thing I remember is standing in the masters' church and someone asking us to join hands in prayer. There was no way could I pray in that building. To me it was the devil's den and I could not take the hand of the white woman standing next to me. Conferring with the black people standing around me, we decided to go outside. When everyone was outside and had made a prayer circle around a huge tree, the folks living nearby came and joined hands with us as prayers were given. During this prayer time the web of hatred began to ease in me and I slowly began to collect my thoughts again. The first thought that crossed my mind was how often people back home asked the question, "where did black folks come from and how did they get here?" I felt the strong need to read every available book and gather all possible information about slavery.

Following our stay in Dakar we took an Air Africa Plane to Sierra Leone. The plane had all-black personnel. From there we went into Freetown by bus. While in Freetown, I had dinner at the home of Mr. and Mrs. Jones, members of the Nova Scotia Descendants Society. Anxious to know something about this society, Mrs. Jones allowed me to see an old minute book. While going through this book, I came to

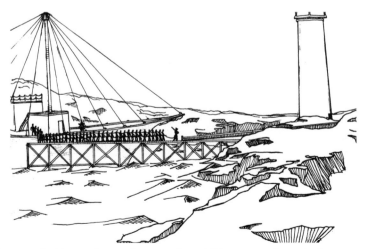

Drawing by Trevor Green, depicting how Africans were brought in chains from the shores of Africa to the New World.

a section that had the 1865 history of the society. Pressed for time, I quickly turned to another section and found the names John Thomas, the great grandson of Jackson, Ellis, Mary Ash, James Turner, David George and others who were listed among the first settlers which arrived in Sierra Leone in 1792, from Nova Scotia. David George and the other settlers organized the first Baptist and Methodist churches in Freetown. These were some of the 1,196 black Loyalists Thomas Peters and his English friend John Clarkson recruited to go to the recently founded colony of Sierra Leone

We left "Kissy" ferry terminal in Freetown and crossed the Atlantic Ocean on a ferry much like the Halifax-Dartmouth ferry. We visited many places in Africa—Court Barrie, Lusar, Nigeria, and Kenya taking in many significant sights such as the many market places, the first black TV networks in Africa, national parks, the hot springs, the parliament building, the safari, and several churches. We received a royal welcome in Court Barri, which is about forty-four miles out of Lusar. When we arrived, our vans were stopped just before we could see what was about to happen. A parade line led by the village chiefs and guided by soldiers on both sides met us as we walked up the road to the crowd of people waving and shouting greetings and welcomes to us. What a wonderful time of meeting and greeting followed by an absolute feast. Returning back to Lansar there was a crowd of people waiting for us at church where a service was given in our honour. I could write a book on the strange and significant sights and events I experienced in Africa: graves adorned with personal belongings of the departed; huge boabab trees; coming so very close to elephants, hippos, hyenas, wildebeest and many other animals. Truly as memorable an Africa experience was my visit to the safari in Kenya as well as to Lake Nakuru National Park, famed for its huge flamingo population. I didn't see many lions or leopards but did see giraffe, zebra, and wildebeest.

To step foot on Sierra Leone soil, knowing that descendants of Nova Scotia had taken some soil with them in 1792 to sprinkle on these grounds, gave me a sense of a common denominator between there and home, thus making this visit the "trip of a life time." It created travel fever in my bones and I continued to travel to many places thereafter. The knowledge and experience I gained through travel could never had been accomplished through any amount of study. I always arrived back home to unwind and share my stories from abroad with family and friends.

Unfortunately, my homecoming after a Caribbean cruise I took in November 1992 wasn't so happy. Arriving at Lester B. Pearson International Airport in Toronto on my way home, I received a message to call home. I was told of Aunt Annie's death and that Mumma had been taken to Hants Community Hospital in Windsor. Needless to say, my flight into Halifax was spent in deep thought about the time I spent with Mumma a couple of days before my cruise. At the time of my visit with her she didn't appear to be her normal self. She seemed to be in a world of her own. This thought I shared with Mona before I left home and also with my friend Madeline while on board the cruise ship. I realized Mumma was eighty-eight years old, and the death of her sister Annie, leaving Mumma the last surviving member of her immediate family, must really have taken its toll on her. Upon my arrival home, Cordell was waiting to take me to the hospital. Here I found Mumma on a life support machine and family members gathered in a waiting room at the hospital. I returned to the car to pull myself together and ask God to help me. Returning to Mumma's bedside, holding her hand and whispering a prayer, I felt a sense of sweet relief come over me and I knew Mumma's time here was over. A day later, on November 30, 1992, Mumma passed away and once again the cold sting of death was upon me. There was a terrible snow storm the day of the funeral and a white blanket of snow covered Mumma's coffin as it was being lowered into the grave. It brought back memories of John's favourite hymn, "Whiter that Snow, Whiter than snow; wash me and I shall be whiter than snow." My faith in God had brought me through again and I found consolation in knowing that even though I was now an orphan and a widow, I was still one of God's children.

In the late 1970s, our church, like many churches, had started to undergo some changes—some thought to the detriment of the moral and ethical standards we aimed to uphold. It seemed that honour and prestige could be maintained within church and community regardless of conduct. Elders started to feel they were not receiving their due respect and that their voices weren't being heard. The interest of other members was drifting away. In the early eighties, financial issues threatened to divide the Preston Church congregation. An annual membership fee of ten dollars was introduced—those who paid were considered active members and could hold office; those who didn't were considered inactive members and could not hold office. On principle, some members, myself included, refused to pay ten dollars; we though it made the church seem like a club that could be joined. We continued to pay our regular tithes and offerings. Church members were slowly leaving our congregation to join churches outside their community. Many tried hard to keep harmony among our membership, but the strength that comes through unity seemed to be fading.

I found this time very difficult and hard to understand. It seemed to me that a person could break every one of God's commandments during the week yet believe it was a mortal sin not to attend church on Sunday. They could cause all the trouble they liked and not be a troublemaker; lie about anything and not be a liar; steal what they wanted and not be a thief; commit adultery and not be an adulterer; sin and not be a sinner. The status quo seemed to be to dress up and go to church on Sunday. Community recognition and prestige appeared to be based on church attendance. While serving as president of the Ladies Auxiliary from 1985-87, I began to feel that a few members were trying to take full control of our church. They saw it as their own, personal church rather than as belonging to the community. And it seemed to me that for some people, God was not everybody's God but their own God. These attitudes were hard for me and for many others to accept. Fortunately, whatever the church was going through, the majority of its members remained and kept the church doors open.

Changes were still taking place in the church in 1995 when Rev. Glenn Gray became pastor. As a matter of fact, some members were rapidly slipping from their own religious belief. On a grey Palm

invisible shadows

Sunday in 1998, while some churches in the area were recalling the biblical account of the waving of palm breaches in the streets of Jerusalem when people heard Jesus was coming (John, chapter twelve), Preston's church congregation was confronted with dissension. As the story goes, just as the Palm Sunday morning service was about to begin, Reverend Glenn Gray walked to the front of the church and announced his resignation as pastor of Preston Church. Then he and his wife walked out of the church. Many eyes filled with tears as some deacons, choir members, and office bearers followed suit. Families split, some husbands walked out while their wives remained, some wives walked out while their husbands remained. The church walk-out took approximately one-half of the congregation with it. The church was left pastorless. (This was not the first, but rather the third, division Preston Church experienced. In 1856, a group left First Preston Church to form South Church, and in 1869, Reverend Thomas left the pastorate.) This split came as a shock to the community. Many residents could not understand what was happening in our church. However, it soon became evident that a search for a new pastor was necessary. Some months later, Reverend Ogueri Ohanaka became Preston's ninth church clergyman.

When I came to live in Preston I found that values carried great weight in the black community and, therefore, good leaders were elected. Their leadership led to the building of community schools, a community post office, and a social centre. These leaders felt a responsibility to their community and held high expectations for accomplishment. Aside from elected leaders, the community had many informal leaders, traditionally played by elders. The deaths of many of the aged left something of the past unremembered. The vivid recollections of the oral tradition, which was established in most black households, was often sustained by elder folk who remembered and never tired of telling of generations gone. When such an elder passes on, the past becomes that much more obscured. When the elders reflected on their life's experiences, it brought a feeling of closeness among the black family. These stories built the bonds of sentiment that kept black people together.

Traditionally, community participation in the decisions made by leaders was important. Interpersonal relationships formed an important element of the quality of life in Preston. The traditional church assumed that all community members were neighbours and it was a norm to maintain friendly neighbourhood ties. Leadership came from the church and one of the church's rules forbid any deep-rooted hatred for fear it would erode community bonds.

In the late 1960s and 1970s there was a black consciousness cultural group of mainly young people rising up in the black community. In 1966, when Stokely Carmichael of the United States announced what he called "Black Power," young people learnt to utter that heretofore unutterable word "black." Although in the 1970s black consciousness was still in an early stage, many of these youth took on a new communal identity, "black people." It was funny but exciting to see how people who spent more than two hundred years greasing and straightening their hair with hot irons had suddenly converted to big Afros. Everyone under thirty-five or so sported an Afro, wore African dashikis, and greeted each other with "brother" and "sister." Young people could be heard reciting, "Say it out loud, I'm black and I'm proud." Of course, the older black generation perceived this change as disrespectful of tradition and believed that it was going to create chaos. These older people were content in their "coloured" neighbourhoods, going to their "coloured" church and school, dating and marrying their own colour. Younger residents who stayed in Preston during the 1970s began to challenge community elders and a battle for leadership ensued. A select few organized various groups, appointing themselves the officers and using the community for fund-raising purposes. By the time the eighties rolled around, this little group had every organization mentionable in place and they had slid into church positions slicker than a cat on a greased tin roof. In their efforts to become the mouthpiece for the community, they ended up silencing most of it.

The new "leaders" limited the community as a whole from participating in the decision-making process in matters that affected their lives. These leaders had a tendency to interact with no more than a few

invisible shadows

family members and a couple of extremely good friends. Business meetings were secretly held in private homes and parts of these in-house meetings were spoon fed to the community at large, if and when members of the group deemed it necessary.

Preston's surrounding communities were extending and growing. Department and large grocery chain stores, fast food chains, gas stations, and several other outlets were moving into Westphal, which was itself rapidly becoming a small town. Westphal's boundaries once again stretched out to reach the Little Salmon River Bridge. The new 107 Highway was put in, by-passing Preston. Porter's Lake, on the other end of Preston, had a small shopping centre. Next door was Lake Echo, which was hastily growing into a large residential area with subdivisions going up all over the place. Preston was left behind, cut-off and squeezed in the middle with its community facilities disappearing fast. Before 1980, Preston had lost its post office, school, and small grocery stores and the recently built Centennial Hall was badly in need of repairs. Several community residents, especially young people, were moving to Toronto, Montreal, and Halifax. Those left in the community were still having very little contact with the outside world. People who had not been in the community long enough to adequately put the community's needs in perspective were being pushed to the front lines as decision makers. Others used the community as a springboard for self prestige. This was an era when a new range of leadership was in place and government grants were flourishing with very little, if any, accountability given. There was simmering resentment at what many saw as corruption among the community's ruling elite and community spirit became drained. Community democracy held little appeal for the residents. At the time there were about three hundred households in Preston but only thirty people attended public meetings. Because Preston was not well organized in terms of its socio-economic structure, the few benefiting from our political paralysis were those being fattened on the crumbs of patronage while holding the greater majority as a captive people that lacked community democracy. To me, thinking that every settlement has its own uniqueness, yet not quite understanding the strange uniqueness of Preston, the present or the future wasn't looking very bright.

During the 1990s a new group of young-blooded Prestonians started to bring back a feeling of pride and hope to the community. They were duly elected as community representatives for the Rate Payers Association, a group that works hand in hand with elected officials. This new group started talking back to the hand-picked community leaders, making it clear that they would not be dictated to and that the community as a whole would set their own priorities. The hand-picked leaders became threatened and their bitterness overflowed to the point that they started manipulating innocent community residents. They created an illegal group to overthrow the elected community representatives. When this illegal group mustered the support of some church officers and preyed on a few senior citizens, they went on the biggest ego and power trip in the history of Preston. They took the duly elected representatives to the Supreme Court under a charge of illegal community organization. On the day of the trial, the group had their supporters in the courtroom to hear the judge's decision; I believe victory prayers and a party were to take place. However, the judge decided against the group and held them financially responsible for court costs. They left the court house still unwilling to claim their own defeat.

In 1992, the Nova Scotia Provincial Legislature created the provincial legislative riding of Preston. This new seat was struck to enhance the chance of a black person being elected to the Nova Scotia House of Legislative Assembly. The riding included the largest black population in Nova Scotia, which consists of the communities of East Preston, North Preston, Cherry Brook, and Lake Loon. During the 1993 provincial election, Wayne Adams was elected the Liberal MLA for this newly cut Preston seat, known as the "Black Seat," and became the first black member of the Nova Scotia Provincial Legislature.

Yvonne Atwell beat Adams in the March 1998 provincial election. Atwell was elected as the NDP MLA for the Preston riding. Although the Preston riding seat was created to enhance the black presence in the Nova Scotia House of Legislative Assembly, this presence was short lived. In the provincial election of July 1999, David Hendsbee (the white candidate) defeated Atwell and slid into the so-called "Black Seat" faster than lightning. It was goodbye to black enchantment!

In 1995, the county councillor position became open as Preston became part of the Halifax Super City. Preston area community identity was destroyed in 1995 when the Nova Scotia Utility and Review Board supported Bill Hayward's plan for a twenty-three-seat Super City council which then divided sections of this community for the sake of numbers. Originally the board had said it wanted no more than a twenty per cent change from the average voting population in a district. Hayward created a Preston-Porter's Lake district which split Cherry Brook/Lake Loon from North and East Preston. At the time, my son, Wendell Thomas, president of East Preston Ratepayers Association, put forth a recommendation for a Preston District Riding. This riding would keep the black communities of Cherry Brook/Lake Loon and North and East Preston together. It would also include areas such as Montague Mines, Humber Park, Westphal Trailer Court and Lake Major. The population of the Preston District Thomas recommended would be about sixty-five per cent black. This recommendation was not accepted; therefore, the county councillor's voting district population is larger than that of the provincial seat and has a majority of white voters, which makes the prospect of having another black councillor doubtful.

So here we are on the brink of the year 2002, when black people should be working together in a movement to fight for equality and our feelings keep us apart. For these past fifteen years I have stopped being the idealist I once was. I realize that if we Preston Blacks ever want to achieve the real things in life and move away from handouts and begging, we must create a new generation of people who will set aside their differences and come together as one united voice; maybe not because they love one another, but because black people still need each other to survive. There is growing evidence of this need today as we look around and see, "the more things change the more they remain the same."

When I look back at the way I had categorized the world I lived in, I think about how I saw my internal world only and not my skin colour.

I never realized how the racial and economic tensions and cultural differences would affect me in the larger society. The black world and the white world are two different places: that's reality. Making sense of that reality and my place in it has been a lifetime process. I often feel squeezed like a lemon in a discriminating society. These forms of discrimination keep my world shattered and cracked, though I have learnt to cut myself some slack, learnt to accept that paradox is part of life. Being able to see two opposites existing side by side has been a source of energy and I expect I will always look for and see them.

Racism against black people comes in many forms. The most open form is guttural racism, which comes with overt language and is considered vulgar—literally low class. Then there is the racism of well-meaning white people who travel in educated circles and carry the attitude of a good concerned citizen when people of colour are present. This group of people is caught in the crossfire between a desire to move beyond "skin deep" and the fear of reprisal from their peers and from society. Institutionalized racism has set black people apart from white society. It exists in education, health care, police departments, political parties and all other institutions created by white people. This form of racism is as hard to root out as a needle in a haystack. These are the forms of racism white people don't want to really discuss, and black people can't stop discussing.

All my life I have been an inquisitive person. I don't know if this comes from being the seventh child or not. Every day I wanted to learn something, but in my day children didn't ask questions like they do today. Every time I tried, I never got the answers I was looking for. So I searched for my answers in books. When I had my family, my reading was done in the late evenings when my children were tucked in bed for the night and John was watching T.V. Also, I sometimes read while rocking my babies to sleep. Many times while ironing or kneading bread I would think back to things I had read and experienced about my race of people and ask the question, "Why?"

Why was Viola Desmond fined and thrown in jail in New Glasgow for refusing to sit in the Jim Crow balcony at Roseland Theatre in 1946? Why, in 1968, was the bylaw that read "Not any Negro nor any Indian shall be buried in St. Croix Cemetery" upheld and a black child refused burial in the cemetery? Why did it take until 1954 for legal segregation of schools in Nova Scotia to end and have segregated schools really closed? The black community of North Preston has its own elementary school. However, the students are bussed a fair distance out of the community to attend an integrated school for junior high. Yet, white children from the immediate surrounding area have never been bussed into North Preston Elementary School. Why is it that all integrated schools are in the white communities? Why did the old folks' desire to stay clustered together in this struggling community of Preston, with barely any awareness of a world beyond this local community's boundaries? Why were community residents not actively involved in political organizations and experiencing both political and economic power?

Unlike most community residents, I was not born thinking about race. Race remained a relative abstraction for me during my childhood. However, I now find myself wondering why race had caused so much hatred within our society. Unfortunately the people I talked to had few answers, and the "whys" stay with me. After hearing so many stories from my friends about their plight in life, I realize Preston's history goes back a long way and so I too had to journey back in time.

My journey of discovery has brought me from childhood and taken me back in time to the era when black men, women and children were white people's property. The time when my black ancestors came off slave ships in neck chains and leg irons, sold from auction blocks like cattle and became nothing more than instruments to the whites of that time. Many carried the mark of the whip on their body as they laboured endlessly in plantation fields. My journey has uncovered reflections on past struggles and successes of our ancestors that helped fashion the black community we live in today. It has brought some shadows from the past and has shed some light, not only on the battle of oppression, racism and neglect, which the black community has endured to reach its present stand, but also on the need for "self-examination."

Hard work and government grants have pushed us ahead a little, yet our eyes still remain on the slave ships that brought our ancestors from the shores of Africa. But maybe it's time to change our focus.

How long do we plan to stand in the same spot, looking back at the chains of slavery, the master's whip and dreaming of the pain they inflicted upon our race. Let's take our share of blame for what we have done to each other and get on with doing something for our community to accomplish our present and future needs. Let's not remain at the border between the work of progress and the world of decay reminding others of the moral and political sins of their forefathers. Let's remove the entrenched jealous hatred among our own black race.

I don't know how much farther my journey is going to take me, but my stop here in Preston has brought me closer to other descendants of former slaves. We are fifth- and sixth-generation Canadians with a history of helping to build our great country. The past struggles and successes of our ancestors can be used as a road map to speed up our journey toward a better world for future generations.

Today Preston is a very different community than existed three centuries ago. Nice houses, all manner of motor vehicles and radio, telephones, television and computers have created communication with the outside world. Amongst all this growth, community residents have much to be thankful for, yet it continues to be a little bit different than most. For some strange reason, far too many community residents cannot relate to the advantages of unity. Although time has changed some things, it has not, cannot and will not change the need for black allegiance and unity. As in the days of old, "together we stand, divided we fall."

Even now, much remains to be known about Preston's early history and it is difficult to guess whether its flower-covered fields and its hills as majestic as when the land was born will be left untouched as in the past or be lost under industries or the streets of a new town.

Appendix A

From Chamberlain's report, September 30, 1815:

Names	Acres Cleared	Remarks
Jacob Claton	1/4	An old man
Jacob Wise	1/4	Able man
Henry Grosse	1/4	Hut partly built
Geo Smith	1	
Peter Claton		No improvements
Danl Taylor		1/2 House built
Richd Grnt	1	Hut built
Nath Johnson	1/2	No hut built
James Downing	3/4	Hut
Solomon Crawley	3/4	Hut
Cal Cooper	1/2	Hut
Peter Duncan		Hut built
Anthony Honeycutt	1/4	House built
Nim Carter		Idle man
Jas. Slaughter	1/2	Hut partly built
Gabb Johnson	1/4	Hut
Jacob Williams	3/4	No hut
Jack Thompson	3/4	Hut
Jno Nelson	3/4	Hut
WM. Dear	3/4	Hut
Abram Ross	1/2	House
WM. Smith	1/2	House
George Brown	1/2	Hut
Ralph Toliver	3/4	Hut
Jerred Thomas		No hut built and doing nothing

In the houses with the other Negroes

WM. Brown

Joseph Glasgo

John Grant and others.

From Chamberlain's report May 9, 1816:

Names	Women	Children
Thomas Saunders	1	3
Peter Layton	1	1
Nat Crawley	1	2
Leven Winder	1	
Henry Bisker		
Henry Taylor	1	1
Charles Wise	1	5
Solomon Crawley	1	2
Geo. Brown	1	4
Betsey Grass		5
Jack Thomson	1	1
Richd Grass		
James Slaughter	1	2
Danl Clayton	1	1
Danl Johnson	1	4

(From Public Archives and Records Management;
the Establishment of ▨▨▨▨ in Nova Scotia, Ferguson.)

invisible shadows